M000214929

Strategies in Workers' Compensation

Richard E. Sall

Health Sciences Library
University of Saskatchewan Libraries
Room B205 Health Sciences Building
107 WIGGINS ROAD
SASKATOON, SK S7N 5E5 CANADA

APR 2 0 2005

Hamilton Books
an imprint of
UNIVERSITY PRESS OF AMERICA,® INC.
Dallas • Lanham • Boulder • New York • Oxford

LIBRARY

Copyright © 2004 by
Richard E. Sall

Hamilton Books
4501 Forbes Boulevard
Suite 200
Lanham, Maryland 20706
UPA Acquisitions Department (301) 459-3366

PO Box 317
Oxford
OX2 9RU, UK

All rights reserved
Printed in the United States of America
British Library Cataloging in Publication Information Available

Library of Congress Control Number: 2004100811
ISBN 0-7618-2771-4 (paperback : alk. ppr.)

∞™ The paper used in this publication meets the minimum
requirements of American National Standard for Information
Sciences—Permanence of Paper for Printed Library Materials,
ANSI Z39.48-1992

Contents

Prologue

Theodore Roosevelt

(Paris, Sorbonne 1910)

"It is not the critic who counts, not the one who points out how the strong man stumbled or how the doer of deeds might have done them better. The credit belongs to the man who is actually in the arena, whose face is marred with sweat and dust and blood; who strives valiantly; who errs and comes short again and again; who knows the great enthusiasms, the great devotions, and spends himself in a worthy cause; who, if he wins, knows the triumph of high achievement; and who, if he fails, at least fails while daring greatly, so that his place shall never be with those cold and timid souls who know neither victory nor defeat."

—"The Man in the Arena"

Introduction

The greatest part of a writer's time is spent in reading, in order to write: A man will turn over half a library to make one book. . . .

—James Boswell, *Life of Samuel Johnson* (1791)

Penned with the Healthcare Medical Professional in mind, the hope is that this book will provide an invaluable source of material for any individual who deals on a daily basis with the injured worker. Human resource professionals, insurance adjusters, case managers, and nurses might well discover the information contained in this manuscript to be an immeasurably useful resource in confronting the myriad of problems that arise within their respective professional fields.

The prime impetus for this undertaking was that of offering reference material to fulfill the comprehensive need for improving upon our summary understanding of the Workers' Compensation system, and the vast potential afforded those of us employed in the field of Occupational Medicine to formulate recommendations and foster implementation of revisions and reform to the current system. Healthcare medical professionals are responsible for determining whether a given patient has sustained a work-related injury or illness, in addition to generating its accompanying activities, such as ordering diagnostic studies and treatment modalities. In assuming these critically important roles, they also are subjected to the assignation of blame for having perpetrated the high costs associated with medical care. Studies have nonetheless revealed that an only a small percentage of patients, from 5 to 20 percent, are responsible for generating the major proportion of costs in medical care, from 80 to 90 percent. Surprisingly, the majority of these patients are not comprised of those individuals presenting with traumatic injury, amputations, or predominant loss of functional capacity but, rather, are constituted by those who, oftentimes, present with ill-defined illnesses, lacking positive physiological findings, and for which unsuccessful response to treatment is frequently evidenced. In many instances, these patients will attempt to and often succeed at achieving protracted and lengthy treatment methods, offering little in the way of benefit at symptom relief, and undergoing an unremitting series of testing procedures. At times, in discovering that a problem necessitates surgical correction, these patients will often continue to remain unimproved following such procedures, and are then frequently the major source of frustration to the Healthcare Provider. Identified as the "difficult patients in Workers' Compensation," a discussion of management techniques for strategically maneuvering through and successfully navigating this somewhat treacherous terrain is provided within the text of this book.

The chapter headings are self-explanatory, amply descriptive of their contents. While the scope of this text is not intended as an all-encompassing panacea for the wide-ranging canvas that comprises management-based problems, it is rather a means by which to offer in-depth discussion of the related issues in an informed and logical manner. In many instances, no one solution exists to a particular problem. Rather, a commingling of both sound judgment and abundant experience conjoin in order that circumstances dictate the optimum course of action toward achieving the best-possible results.

I would like to express my appreciation for all the wonderful people I have worked with throughout my career, for their assistance and insight. A special thanks is offered to Dr. William Greaves, M.D., for both his review of the material and valued recommendations, and to my patient and talented editor, Wendy Reis, of Phantom Court Publishing. Others who were involved in assisting me in this enterprising endeavor include my wife Rita, and friends who provided valuable review and comments during its creation.

Chapter One

The History of Occupational Medicine

. . . . I may venture to add one more question: What occupation does he follow?

—Dr. Bernardo Ramazzini (1700)

HISTORY

Originally discovered amongst slaves who performed stonecutting for the pyramids of Egypt, silicosis was the first identified occupational disease, while the second identified occupational disease is considered that of Farmer's Lung (hypersensitivity pneumonitis), generally associated with grain harvesting and domestication activities. Despite careful observance of the causes of ill health by ancient physicians, the myriad effects relative to an individual's occupation as a causative element of disease were often ignored. This negligence might perhaps be attributable to the preponderance of labor performed by those inhabiting the lower-strata of society, predominantly comprised of slaves and prisoners, and thus considered to be of no social value or merit. These slaves and prisoners were relegated to low-level, unskilled tasks that accrued little or no benefits, and thus accorded little or no attention paid to accompanying maladies suffered as consequence of these activities.

In his published work *De Morbis Artificum* (Italy, 1700), Dr. Bernardino Ramazzini first identified and categorized Occupational Disease, the data of which was gathered from his observations of workers engaged in cleaning public cesspools. Having noted that gastroenteritis was endemic to this population of workers, Ramazzini identified the existing link between their chosen occupation and its accompanying symptomatology. In another edition of this work, published in 1713, Ramazzini further stated:

> *The maladies that affect the clerks aforesaid arise from three causes. First, constant sitting, secondly, the incessant movement of the hand, and always in the same direction, thirdly, the strain on the mind from the effort not to disfigure the books by errors or cause loss to their employers when they add, subtract, or do other sums in arithmetic. The diseases brought about by sitting constantly are easily understood; they are obstructions of the viscera, e.g., the liver and spleen, indigestion in the stomach, numbness of the legs, a considerable hindrance of the circulation of the blood, and an unhealthy habit.* (163)

The above quote clearly indicates that Ramazzini is here referring to clerical work in which little or no exercise is either permitted or voluntarily engaged in by the employees. The repetition of hand motions over a period of long duration, in combination with sitting in one position for extended periods can cause numbness of the limbs, and other painful symptoms or syndromes. This, then, added to the growing knowledge of the linkage between occupational exercises and disease, and how the two in combination can work toward creating ill health.

The number of occupations that have been profiled which pose a relationship between physical, health-oriented, and environmental risks and workers has shown an increase from 55 during Ramazzini's era to numbers greater than 5,000 currently, adding to a growing record of data that supports the need for, design of, and implementation of programs and protocols for occupational medicine created to enhance and supplement worker safety and health.

EARLY AMERICA

Colonial America can be characterized in terms of a scarcity of skilled workers and high wage rates for those highly trained laborers. Americans possessing high-level skills and training backgrounds were paid on the average as much as three times that of the wages paid to similarly-skilled workers in England. In accordance with a need for highly skilled workers, free housing and land were proffered to English workers, such as carpenters and shoe-makers, both willing and able to migrate to America in order to fill the deep-ening gap between supply and demand evidenced during this era. The impor-tation of labor would ultimately lead to a transformation in this dire situation following the American Revolution, greatly impacting future methods for the organization, coordination, and control of work environments.

The emergent factory system, characterized by large-scale mechanization and a climate of increased competitiveness, both domestic and foreign, re-sulted in a somewhat unstable economy. Innovative technological advance-ments worked toward promoting either the downscaling or total elimination of many skilled positions, diminishing the dignity and pride of workmanship traditionally associated with the labor market. This propelled a loss of com-munity status and economic insecurity alike amongst workers, leading to an increase in hostilities experienced by labor and the burgeoning development of trade unions.

Amid this new environment, workers found themselves at a distinct disad-vantage. The tide of an unprecedented wave of immigration witnessed be-tween the years 1870 and 1914 afforded employers an overabundant pool of unskilled laborers from which to choose, most of whom were both willing and able to endure long working hours, extremely harsh working conditions, and meager wages. Adding to the instability and uncertainty of the times was the volatile nature of an economy that resulted in both wage cuts and sporadic employment (164, 165).

The uniquely American concept of trade unions as they exist in their pres-ent format originated during the 1880s, with the development of its legal framework established during the 1930s. In its earliest stages, workers joined these unions in large part for monetary and safety purposes. Today, however, the majority of employees join unions, for the most part, due to some level of dissatisfaction or grievance with either their job status or underlying eco-nomic conditions, or both, as well as a need and desire to acquire a greater measure of influence over work-related issues and environmental conditions in the workplace.

THE INDUSTRIAL REVOLUTION

The era of American industrialization, falling between the periods of the Civil War and World War I, produced hazardous and unsanitary working conditions throughout many industries. A dearth of regulatory policies and laws existed, with factory inspectors sadly deficient in the enforcement of the scant legal measures that had been enacted. Women and children were often grievously exploited, similar in many ways to the present working conditions found to exist and constantly monitored amongst the status of workers throughout Third-World Countries today. During the 1880s, for example, it became evident that Byssinosis, a disease characterized by tightness of the chest, shortness of breath, and accompanied by wheezing, was endemic amongst those who were employed as cotton workers in the textile industry.

Overly long working hours, along with intolerable working conditions, combined with poor sanitary systems and deplorable housing arrangements, to result in drastic increases in both the quantity and types of occupational diseases found to exist amongst many workers. Child labor practices sprung from the need for employers to obtain lowest-cost labor possible, with children coming not only cheaply but also submissively under the reign of employers. With child labor practices in place, little if any danger existing of union organization, either amongst individual workers or as cohesively organized trade unions for the purpose of improving working conditions and environments, higher pay scales, or both. A large variety of occupations within the textile industry proved to be less expensive to employ two children at a rate of $3.00 per week than to employ either a man or woman in the same position for higher wage levels. The pronounced use of child labor was greatly bolstered by the needs of the textile industry to turn profits in the most cost-effective manner.

An investigative study, conducted by the United States Census Bureau in 1905, included approximately 3,297,819 workers and noted that average earnings totaled $10.06 per week, with male workers over the age of 16 earning an average of $11.16 per week, while those below the age of 16 averaged a rate of $3.46, and women earned at an average rate of $6.17 per week, cementing the validity of data as indicated above: children fared the poorest in terms of earnings averages per week, while adults commanded higher pay scales, leading employers to continue to rely upon child labor to both increase their profit margins and exploit the submissive nature of children.

The rates of accidents amongst workers continued to increase during this period, peaking to an all-time high in 1907. Although the National Association of Manufacturers was in direct opposition to laws introduced prohibiting child labor practices, minimum wage rates and maximum working hours per day, the public at-large lent its support to aid those labor groups seeking the enactment of this legislation following the period of 1900 (155), in the Progressive Era. The demonstrated support for prohibition of child labor practices paved the road to newly-created governmental regulation that specifically addressed worker safety and occupational health-related issues. These laws sought to overcome the multiple shortcomings of factory-related legislation and enforcement through the introduction of two innovative strategies, that of Workers' Compensation and the general oversight of these strategies to be executed by the formation of industrial-based commissions.

The end of the era of the "assumed risk" doctrine, that of the ingeniously-devised process of reasoning holding that a servant is permitted to quit his or her job if one considers it to be of a hazardous nature; yet, should that self-same servant choose to retain that job, and is subsequently killed in the pursuit of activities ensuing to that job, having assumed such hazard, the employer can then not be held liable for his or her death. The logic inhering to this doctrine was based on the premise that the employer could not be held accountable for any death of a given servant, as it was at the sole discretion of the servant to forgo this position prior to accident, and given all opportunities to do so.

The basis for this concept derived from an 1837 English law, whereby Fowler, an English butcher, ordered his servant Priestly to ride on a van that contained meat scheduled for delivery. Although leveling complaints to his employer that the van was overburdened with goods, Priestly nonetheless did as he was ordered and boarded the van. The van ultimately broke down, crushing Priestly's leg, for which he later brought lawsuit against his boss. The employer's defense was handled by Lord Abinger, who successfully defended the case by arguing that the injury resulted from the fault of the fellow servant driving the van, thus the risk was assumed by those who accepted the work, and not through employer negligence.

In 1841, the above falsely-based premise was used with success in the United States, allowing both "assumed risk" and "fellow servant" theories to deprive thousands of individuals of appropriate monetary benefits for work-related injuries.

THE COMPANY DOCTOR

During the era of the American frontier, those employers operating railroad, lumber, and mining industry operations in often remote geographic locations found it necessary to make arrangements for basic medical services to minister to the frequent medical emergencies and work-related injuries existent among their labor populations. Immigrant laborers, often employed in these dangerous trades, were traditionally overworked and underpaid for their services, willing to accept any available tasks offered, performing the heavy, hot, dirty, and hazardous labor activities necessary in the development of pioneer

America. Those who lost their lives in the mining disasters, construction trades, or steel mills of America were oftentimes predominantly comprised of foreign-born individuals. The physicians who practiced during this era were most often employed in private practice, customarily administering treatment to accident victims either directly at on-site work locations, or in their regionally-located offices and local hospitals. As was the case most frequently, these doctors were inadequately trained, with remuneration allocated on a piecemeal basis. Despite having experienced generally negative results with these "company" physicians, there existed a group of several physicians who contributed considerably in positive ways to the treatment of steel mill, factory, and mining workers during this period (135). The following quote, as conveyed by an article in the *The Free Lance* newspaper, dated 5 September 1902, is testament to those physicians willing to positively impact the lives and work-related conditions of laborers during this nascent period of American frontier development:

A frightful accident resulting in the death of Alvias Smith occurred here on Friday evening. Shepard Brothers, timber contractors for the Annie Laurie Mine, had just completed a chute from the Marysvale Road down the mountainside towards the mill. The logs run on the ground and are guarded by a log wall on either side. Alvias Smith, Warren Moody, and a third man, were working near the chute and well down the hill. They were at liberty, indeed expected, to quit work at ten minutes to six in the evening. Their failure to do so cost Smith his life. The whistle blew but the men continued their work. Bert Shepard, inferring that the men had left, started a log down the chute. Rain had wet the ground and the log moved almost noiselessly down on its errand of death. Moody heard the log jump the chute, glanced up the hill, dropped and called "duck" to the men just below him. Smith, instead of "ducking," started to run. The flying log caught him just behind and above the left ear and crushed his skull. . . . The unconscious man was taken to the hospital, where Dr. Kjaerbye thought the case was hopeless. Thomas Smith, his father, arrived and urged that an operation be performed. Dr. Lyon, having the same opinion as Dr. Kjaerbye, performed the operation but the patient died some two or three hours afterward. A coroner's inquest was suggested, but a careful investigation by the father of the deceased and several friends convinced them that no one was to blame, therefore the formality of an inquest was dispensed with.

The newly-enacted State Workers' Compensation laws lent acknowledgment to the concept that work is inevitably hazardous, thus replacing the moral and legal tenets of individual fault with those of socially responsible policy — thus, assigning the costs associated with accidents to the employer, to ultimately become the more normal cost of conducting business operations in America. Should a work-related activity possess an inherently dangerous or hazardous element to it, the cost of work-related injuries potentially resulting from this type of activity falls to the employer, not the employee.

In combination with the increase in work-related accident rates, and the advent of Workers' Compensation legislation, medical practice in the workplace found itself transformed in parallel to these changes as well. Apart from the treatment of work-related injuries, the role of medical practitioners experienced a radical metamorphosis. The Industrial Safety Movement, adopted by engineers, was born, the role of which was the general oversight of accident prevention. The single health-related activity for which medicine could claim exclusive jurisdiction and license was that of the certification of health status (136).Between the years 1900 and 1915, physician services increased, necessitated by the need to verify the legitimacy of accident and work-related claims of injury, resulting in measurable growth in the field of industrial medicine.

Despite safety engineer assistance in the reduction of accident prevalence, recognition was now paid to the notion that passive protection was but only one element necessary in efforts to reduce work-related injuries. The creation of a safety-conscious and educated workplace environment was perceived to be central to any methods and strategies aimed at safety, the most important objective of which was to convince employees of the genuine concern possessed by employers for their general well-being and welfare. In that vein, a factory-based medical program, well-staffed by highly qualified and trained physicians, can serve as both a symbol and agent of employer concern for worker health and safety.

Programs of periodic worker examinations fast developed to become the cornerstone of occupational medicine practices, enhancing its ability to detect those individuals deemed to possess health deficits and could then be categorized and transferred to jobs better suited to both their physical liabilities and capabilities. This, then, satisfied the need for the concept of fitting the specific individual to the specific job.

In 1932, the American Medical Association (AMA) voiced considerable criticism of corporate medical practices as being socialistic in nature, stating that contractual practice of medicine as compared to independently-operating private medical practitioners, transformed physicians into nothing more than hirelings for the sole purpose of administering to individuals in a robotic fashion. This criticism was directly applicable to those practicing in the area of industrial medicine, in turn providing more fuel to the longstanding antagonistic relationship existing between occupational medicine and the AMA. Consequently, in the course of submitting their applications to the AMA for board certification, practitioners in the field of occupational medicine were denied certification in 1937, with the AMA stating, "there is no such thing as a specialty of industrial medicine and surgery . . . that this is simply one of the subtopics under general medicine" (137). This tactic of denial was adhered to until 1955, at which time the specialty of Occupational Medicine was finally granted due recognition by the AMA, albeit only acknowledging its creditability as a subdivision of Preventive Medicine.

BOARD RECOGNITION

Prior to gaining the status of board certification, the marginalization of industrial physicians was commonplace, with industrial practitioners being relegated to and grappling with lack of firm structural roles and procedures, either within the business community or the health care industry itself. Operating on the periphery or fringes of the major medical community forced industrial medical practitioners to tolerate the following system deficits:

1. Lack of control or management of both the structure and content of corporate-based medical programs and procedures;
2. Isolation from health care financing within corporate enterprises;
3. Having to assume submissive and subordinate roles and functions in relation to externally-based medical care systems; and,
4. Lacking both meaningful relationships to hospitals and having no influence in the arena of medical school curricula.

The amelioration of the above deficits in the field of Occupational Medicine was brought to bear by the passage of the Occupational Safety and Health Act (OSHA) by Congress in 1970. This Act was the result of a marked increase seen in the rates of worker-related injuries, greater accessibility to and knowledge of occupational diseases and their relationship to productivity in the workplace, measurable growth in the environmental protection movement, and statistically significant changes evidenced in both United States demographics and the expectations of the American labor force (138). The passage of OSHA now cast both government and industry in adversarial roles, thus impelling companies to expend non-productive resources and allocate support for activities related to occupational medical practitioners. In effect, a conversion was evidenced in the field of health conservation from one of a fringe-dwelling, somewhat limited form of medical practice, to that of a legitimatized product of the industrial infrastructure (139). Employee health and safety issues were now considered to be an integral element of every American business enterprise, affecting millions of workers across a wide swath of industrial occupations.

Over the course of the past thirty years, numerous laws and policy regulations have been passed and enacted through Congressional legislation, with the continued growth of occupational medicine now encompassing an ever-widening spectrum of activity. Drug testing procedures in the workplace, disability management techniques and methodologies, and wellness programs of every stripe only identify but a few examples of this burgeoning field. An increasing partnership alliance with the business community has further fostered the advancement and development of Occupational Medicine.

By 1981, radical changes emerged in American corporate culture as an outcome of downsizing, in turn sizably reducing the numbers of both labor and management throughout the business community. Consequently, many corporate health divisions and departments were either reduced in staff or shut down completely, with their activities outsourced to externally-based medical organizations that now assumed these functions. Medical providers who experienced corporate layoffs due to downsizing migrated to either freestanding or hospital-based occupational associations or programs. By shifting corporate providers to external sources, the values and tenets of occupational medicine, previously reflective of jointly-held corporate/governmental/academic cooperative efforts, now instead assumed both the interests and values of independent providers (144).

In 1983, hospitals initiated diversification strategies through the institution of outpatient care services, forming more strongly-held ties with medical payers and, in particular, formulating bonds with employers. Occupational Medicine was well-equipped to fit this newly-emerging medical strategy, as hospitals avidly developed clinics adapted to specialize in this area specifically, and the quantity of these types of facilities soon greatly increased at a rapid pace.

In 1990, the United States was witness to the initiation of government-mandated drug testing, which currently impacts millions of employees throughout the country. The need for this service has also aided in propelling the overall growth and development of occupational medicine. Computer-based technological advancements throughout every industry have also spurred growth rates in the practice of Occupational Medicine, as newly described and identified health and safety concerns emerge at an almost unprecedented rate. The necessity for organizations and corporate structures to integrate both the well-being and health of its workers, along with advancing knowledge and databases of information regarding safety-related issues in the workplace, all serve to further progress the field of Occupational Medicine. Along with these explosive changes and needs as our workplace cultures dramatically change over time and well into the new millennium, it is paramount to understand as well as adapt to these alterations in the way we work and how they impact employment issues both currently and in the future. New dynamics and paradigms for managing and administering the field of Occupational Medicine will have far-reaching effects not only for its practitioners, but for those working in fields directly and indirectly related to workplace health and safety.

Chapter Two

The Workers'
Compensation Environment

What a heavy oar the pen is, and what a strong current ideas are to row in!

—letter to Louise Colet, 23 October 1851, in *Letters of Gustave Flaubert* (1980), Vol. 1 (trans. F. Steegmuller)

LAWS

The Workers' Compensation system, as the longest established American insurance program, was adopted in most states between eighty and ninety years ago. Based upon a no-fault system, this program was designed as a means by which to eliminate litigation in cases for which employers might be held negligent in causing worker-related injuries. Notwithstanding that, these issues have expanded to other areas, such as those regarding whether the injury can be proven to be work-related, or what monetary and other benefits might be accorded the injured worker.

In the United States, Workers' Compensation legislation (33) falls under the jurisdiction of individual states, each with its own respective set of laws. In addition, Federal Workers' Compensation laws encompass all federal employees and citizens of Washington, D.C. as well, including special laws for longshoremen, railroad workers, and coal miners, the intentions of which are listed as follows:

a. Compensation allocated for permanent disability or death from work-related injury;
b. Compensation dispensed for lost wages; and,
c. Provision of both medical care and rehabilitation for injured worker.

Although variance in these laws exists between one state and another (97), they all basically adhere to the following general principles:

The injured worker shall receive all necessary medical care until recovered as much as is possible.

The terminal point of coverage is termed, "Maximum Medical Improvement (MMI).

It is not necessary for the worker to offer proof of employer negligence.

The injury occurred during the course of employment, the likelihood of which is that it occurred during work-related activity than not.

The foundational concept of Workers' Compensation is that no expense will be spared while the worker recovers to the maximum extent possible, based upon the assumption that care will prove both cost-effective and reasonable. Variability in both State and Federal laws include: determination of monetary compensation for lost wages and impairment; the right of the employee to choose a medical provider; access to fee schedules of available medical providers; the role and function of independently operating medical examiners; mental health claims; and, the role played by insurance companies.

Unlike a majority of socially-based insurance programs, such as that of Social Security and Unemployment Compensation, the major portion of Workers' Compensation benefits is administered not by government agency, but primarily under the auspices of private parties, such as insurance companies that are authorized to transact business, and self-insured employers. The functionary role of the State in the benefit delivery system includes oversight of dispensation of benefits, regulation of all parties involved in the system, and management of dispute resolution when deemed necessary.

COMPENSATION

A major percentage of participating States provide lost wage compensation, generally consisting of an amount not to exceed a ceiling of two-thirds salary. These funds are paid until such time as the worker either returns to full-time employment, or for a specified number of weeks, contingent upon the degree of injury.

CHOICE OF PHYSICIAN/MEDICAL PROVIDER

A majority of participating States in the Workers' Compensation program makes allowances for the employee to choose a Medical Provider, while also assuming the right of the employer to choose an alternative physician to determine a second medical opinion, or for further testing and examination procedures. In some instances, several States, such as Ohio, have adopted Managed Care Systems in which employee choice of medical provider is restricted to those provided by the employer or insurer.

A proportion of States accord providers the ability to set their own fees, provided these fees are not deemed excessive, with a major portion of the states possessing fee schedules. Medical fee schedules are utilized in forty-two jurisdictions, primarily functioning as means by which to contain medical costs in Workers' Compensation systems. An evaluation, comparing reimbursements for medical care in these jurisdictions (87), demonstrate a low rate of correlation between fee schedules and costs incurred to deliver medical services (cost-of-living) by healthcare providers to injured workers in various locations (see Appendix, Attachment A). If the schedule of rates is excessively high, the fee program will be less apt to achieve cost containment goals and, conversely, if rates are too low, the accessibility to quality care might be inhibited. The disparity observed between medical fee schedule levels and provider costs raises concerns that States might be either over- or underutilizing medical care services (35).

A logical system of fee schedules should provide for higher reimbursements in those States in which delivery of services incur higher costs, and vice-versa. Currently, under our system, this is not the case across all States participating in Workers' Compensation fee schedule programs. For example, out of the forty States presented in the above study, five of these—Nebraska, Connecticut, Oregon, Alaska, and Idaho—set fee schedules at a rate almost double or triple that of Medicare's rate of reimbursement (see Appendix, Attachment A), while three of these States, that of Florida, Massachusetts, and Maryland, the fee schedules are set either at or below Medicare's mandated reimbursement rate applicable to their respective States. The study demonstrates that 18 of 40 States administer payments above the level of Medicare allowances, and exceed a 100 percent level in at least one major service category. This would indicate a wide disparity between what is required by State law and the enforcement of these regulations as pertains to individual State Workers' Compensation benefit programs.

INDEPENDENT MEDICAL EXAMINATIONS

In those cases for which an independent medical examination might be necessitated or considered prudent, circumstances surrounding a given injury often produce thus-far unanswered questions that create a need for unbiased opinion concerning these issues. These issues might be addressed by determination of the following elements:

a. Verification of worker injury;
b. Medical necessity of treatment;
c. Modification of worker duties and activities as required by level of injury sustained; and,
d. Extent or degree of permanent as compared to temporary impairment to worker.

MENTAL HEALTH CLAIMS

The majority of States place limitations on claims for work-related mental illness, specifically those involving stress-related syndromes and/or depression.

The reason for this was because between 1979 and 1988, job related mental stress claims increased by nearly 700% in California alone (167). After a major overhaul of the California workers' compensation laws in 1993, a new and higher threshold was established for these claims with several restrictions, to prevent healthy people with normal everyday stresses from filing claims.

ROLE OF INSURANCE COMPANIES

Tax-supported Compensation Boards serve the function throughout many States of providing all monetary benefits to workers, and employer-contribution mandated, while in other States employers are required to purchase insurance through private carriers. Furthermore, several States make allowance for larger business enterprises to utilize forms of self-insurance, most cases of which make allowance for third-party administrators to be hired by the employer.

MEDICAL TREATMENT

Acute injury management involves multiple stages, including determination of appropriate diagnosis, setting up timely treatment protocols, the use of specialists where appropriate, and as rapid a return to employment as is possible. At the discretion and option of the employer, most Modified Duty Programs require consultations with employers prior to initiation of program. Chronic disability determined to result from work-related injury occurs in approximately 10 percent of all cases, yet is responsible for the majority of costs associated with these types of injury. Medical treatment modalities of these cases often require a combination of patience, persistence, and practicality.

At such time as the worker has attained Maximum Medical Improvement (MMI), the physician is then required to determine the extent of permanent impairment or disability to that worker. Medical treatment represents approximately 40 percent of total costs associated with Workers' Compensation programs. In order to seek medical care, the employee must be of the belief that he or she has suffered a workplace-related injury. Acceptance of the worker for treatment under the Workers' Compensation system is grounded in the principle that the treatment professional has certified that the worker has in fact been injured.

The certification process is initiated at the workplace or site via the completion of a *First Report of Injury*, required by law and reported on the OSHA-based 300 Log form. The acceptance of an injury forms the underpinning of the agreed-upon contract between the worker and whichever medical care provider he or she requests to administer treatment. The medical provider validates the injury as to whether the injury, in his/her opinion, is work related or not. If work related, a de facto authorization exists for treatment. If not work related, the individual is referred to their private medical provider for treatment. If the injured worker disagrees with opinion of the provider, a second opinion is usually allowed by the insurance company from an independent medical examiner.

QUALITY OF MEDICAL CARE

Issues relating to quality of care within the Workers' Compensation system have been the source of both widespread criticism and focal points for discussion groups. These discussion groups have encountered distrust amongst injured parties, which serves as a barrier to quality care improvement. The intrusive nature of medical and/or legal concerns into the treatment sphere can oftentimes promote the potential for problems. Other areas of concern can include:

a. Lack of familiarity by physicians with the field of occupational medicine; preventive measures and strategies for disability issues; return-to-work issues, as well as the overall Workers' Compensation system and its operational principles.
b. Adequate accessibility to specialty care and other treatment procedures.

c. Inadequate or insufficient data available regarding provider levels of performance.
d. Accountability by both health care providers and insurance carriers in the provision of quality health care.

COSTS

As stated by Dr. Richard Gelberman, President of the American Academy of Orthopedic Surgeons, "musculoskeletal conditions have reached epidemic proportions, costing the U.S. $254 billion annually" (49). Furthermore, a U.S. Department of Labor Report has asserted that the total number of these types of injuries involves one out of seven working people (31).

The total associated costs of work-related injury involve both lost productivity and training expenditures. In addition to medical care costs and lost-time benefits, failure to formulate a proactive approach to the management of employee disability claims can result in spiraling costs that reach out-of-control proportions for business enterprises. It would serve the business culture well to put into place internally-based or on-site systems for the guidance of injured workers throughout the course of their recovery up to and including the final phase of returning to work. A process such as this would not only ensure appropriate medical care, but also provide ongoing interaction between worker and management through the establishment of treatment objectives and expectations. An effectively designed and executed disability management program will protect not merely the bottom-line monetary objectives of a business enterprise, but increase both work performance and productivity of the injured worker.

Often perpetrated by workplace injuries, a defensive posture can often be seen to exist amongst employers who adhere to the notion that both the system and discontent or employees with poor attitudes take advantage of both the company and the accompanying Workers' Compensation program. These attitudes work toward encouraging injured employees to prolong their return to employment, remaining at times absent from their jobs for protracted periods. These employees often harbor sentiments of being misunderstood and underappreciated by their employers, which may or may not be based in truth. A method for counterattacking these sentiments is that, through engaging in extended absences from work, these employees promote an increase in insurance premiums for the employer. Termed the "sick workplace syndrome," this behavior in turn leads to excessive costs and generally poor outcomes. Not the product of an unfair system per se, but rather the result of poorly designed and managed Workers' Compensation programs, along with competing self-interests, this type of conduct contributes to and weighs heavily in creating adversarial employee-employer relations (70), adding substantially to unnecessary and avoidable costs.

Beginning during the latter part of the 1980s, reform measures were introduced and subsequently enacted throughout many States as means to curb the excessive growth witnessed in costs of insurance claims. These newly-enacted laws worked toward providing greater ability for management of medical care costs, treatment protocols, and return-to-work processes for injured workers. The usage of large insurance deductibles induced employers to become more cognizant of safety issues. Reform policies regarding residual market along with reform measures targeting fraudulent activity combined to result in measurable declines in the costs of claims. However, this downward trend is now seen to be leveling off, with losses once again on the rise.

The California Workers' Compensation Insurance Rating Bureau (WCIRB) estimates a combined ratio of 138 for the year 2001, a decrease from the figure of 162 seen in 2000. For every premium dollar that insurers of Workers' Compensation earn, an expenditure of $1.38 is allocated for claims and expenses. Elements that drive these costs in an upward direction include medical care, increasing 11 percent, and payments associated with lost wages, increasing by 6 percent. In California during 2001, the average cost per claim increased to $45,000, partially offset by a continued decline evidenced in the number of claims filed per worker. Nevertheless, investment income, which supplements the revenues earned from premiums, has also shown a marked decline.

HISTORY

At a meeting of the National Commission on State Workers' Compensation Laws, held on July 31, 1972 in Washington, D.C., criticism was leveled at State Workers' Compensation programs, threatening a Federally-administered takeover of these programs should these deficiencies not be corrected (64). Although the National Commission did not convene again, many State insurance programs showed demonstrable improvements in advancing toward the adoption of the Commission's recommendations. An increase in Workers' Compensation benefits as well as new systems for the indexing and categorization of benefits relative to wage increases resulted in dramatically increasing annual costs to employers. Following these changes, annual costs of Workers' Compensation programs have increased from a total of $4.9 billion in 1970 to about $150 billion in 2000 (216).

PROBLEM AREAS

The problems associated with a majority of Workers' Compensation claims can be attributed to lack of accountability protocols. In general, medical providers are accorded unrestricted freedom to order any testing and diagnostic procedures that might prove beneficial to the recovery of the injured worker. Cost efficacy and medical treatment outcome studies have been conducted resulting in the issuance of treatment guidelines, however, these directives have not found universal acceptance by medical providers. Often, as is the case, insurance adjusters are too engaged in other claim processes and frequently overextended in their activities. In all likelihood, 80 percent of litigated claims registered under the Workers' Compensation system reached the stage of legal recourse due to either a lack of or poor communication with the employee, who is often in a state of confusion, both intimidated and measurably frustrated by the system bureaucracy. Many observers have asserted that the legal system and, at times, the State legislatures, are in the process of broadening the scope of coverage for Workers' Compensation and, indeed, they have noted an increase in the types and categories of injury and illness currently allowable under Workers' Compensation as compared to one decade past (29, 30). For example, ergonomically-based injury claims have shown to be on the increase, currently drawing noticeable attention from employers and insurance companies alike. These work-related injuries encompass a wide symptomatology spectrum involving the upper extremities in individuals engaged in the performance of repetitive motion tasks (92). However, the sometimes-nebulous nature of these injuries proves difficult when attempting to determine a pre-existing condition etiology, or ascertain what percentage of the presenting problem to be verifiably work-related.

The legal system appears to be more liberal in its interpretation of those activities that fall within the scope of employment. Conditions considered definitively traceable to workplace events are often covered under Workers' Compensation, although objectively-based tests are not yet available for such symptoms and/or conditions. Workers' Compensation programs are undergoing vast changes by incorporating a broader-scoped vision and liberalization in matters concerning medical provider options, such as the ability of employees to choose amongst a wider array of medical care providers. For example, there have been some pilot programs where the injured employee can self refer to a specialist on a pre-approved list by the insurance company, and it was cost effective. Overall, greater satisfaction with treatment was obtained by the injured workers utilizing this system.

STATISTICAL DATA

Approximately nine out of ten workers in the United States workforce are protected under the provisos of Workers' Compensation Insurance, compulsory for the greater majority of all employees across all States, with the lone exception of Texas, for which a completely optional (voluntary-based) program exists. The most common classes of non-covered employees are casual workers (those who work occasionally or intermittently), domestic servants, some agricultural workers, real estate persons, and certain employees of religious, charitable and other non-profit organizations, and the self employed. If an employee is not covered under a particular state law, and the employer elects no workers' compensation coverage, then the usual tort rules apply between the parties (168).

The National Council on Compensation Insurance (NCCI), which is the premier workers' compensation data repository that serves the insurance industry, attributes the recent decline in frequency of work-related accidents to the expanding use of robots, which works toward measurable reductions in employee exposure to hazardous activity. Power- and electronically-assisted devices serve to reduce human physical stress, are comprised of lighter and stronger materials than in the past, and are equipped with ergonomically-correct design features that strongly reduce human physical strain. Wireless tools and gadgetry have also aided in reducing the rate of incidence of accidents as resulting from individuals tripping over errant wires and cords in the workplace. Additionally, worker safety and technology training have improved considerably over the past few decades. In 2000, a total of 5.7 million injuries and illnesses (31) were recorded throughout private industry workplace environments, of which approximately 2.8 million workers required absence from work and/or restrictive duties and activities while engaged in work. The incidence of lost workday cases has also declined, from 4.1 cases per 100 full-time workers in 1990, to a total of 3.0 cases per 100 in the year 2000, with the lowest rate on record occurring in 2002, at a rate of 1.8 cases per 100 employees.

Of the 362,500 newly-recorded cases of occupational illnesses, 67 percent are categorized under the identifier of repetitive trauma syndrome. One primary benefit issue yet to find resolution in several States is that of the imbalance existing between levels of compensation and the various degrees and extent of impairment; where permanent partial disability has a tendency to be overcompensated while a classification of permanent total disability tends toward being undercompensated throughout the Workers' Compensation system. Benefits in several States can be viewed as inadequate, while considered overgenerous in others.

Health Sciences Library
University of Saskatchewan Libraries
Room 6.08 Health Sciences Building
187 WIGGINS ROAD
SASKATOON, SK S7N 5E5 CANADA

A steep rise in employer costs was evidenced during the 1980s and early part of the 1990s, with a noticeable decline recorded until recent times. During the mid-1950s, private-sector employers expended on-average 0.5 percent of their payroll for Workers' Compensation. Noting the gaping disparity, California's expenditures for the year 2003 for Workers' Compensation contributions totals 5.0 percent (125) of payroll for Workers' Compensation. With expansion of both coverage and concomitant benefits, State legislatures have been placed under increased pressure to seek new methods for reducing employer expenditures for Workers' Compensation.

FRAUD

Workers' Compensation fraud, as defined by California law, is rather simple: "It's illegal to lie to get benefits." Successfully prosecuting these infractions requires the ability to determine first, proving the validity of the lie and, second, willful intent to defraud, both of which might prove difficult to ascertain. Often, insurance company investigators provide videotape presentations of employees to Sonoma County District Attorney, Bruce Enos, who states: "The videos don't prove a lie or criminal intent. The Workers' Compensation system is stacked for legitimate reasons in favor of the worker [to avoid false accusations]."

The Lynch Ryan Report (Spring 1993) asserts that a good number of insurance companies make allowance for fraudulent conduct as being an integral component and thus cost of doing business, with these added costs in turn passed on to customers, stating that:

> *Most people assume that fraud involves primarily workers faking injuries. To be sure, this happens. To find the heart of the fraud problem, however, you must follow the money. And money most often ends up in the hands not of the workers, but the professionals who live off the system: a relatively small percentage of the nation's doctors, lawyers, insurance adjusters, and dishonest employers. While blame falls most often on the shoulders of the worker, we believe that a small minority of professionals make the most money through fraud.*

The most obvious form of employer fraud is terms *Premium Fraud*, whereby more incentives are available to employers to defraud insurers proportionate to the recent sizable increases in coverage rates for Workers' Compensation. Several employers will file false reports regarding both the size and nature of their businesses in order to obtain lower insurance premium coverage. Premium fraud is primarily based upon the methods by which premiums are calculated by insurers. These premium rates are founded on payroll size in which rates are built-in to the equation, higher rates accorded to work-related activities considered to be high-risk in nature. Hundreds of job categories exist, each possessing distinct rates. In order to compute the appropriate rate, accurate data regarding employer payrolls and nature of work performed is needed by insurance companies. Cases exist certainly in which a percentage of employers will intentionally understate either one or both of these data elements.

For example, an employer might identify a particular employee's payroll under the category of clerical in order to lower the premium rate, while another claim is filed for a secretarial employee who fell from a roof. In reality, the individual categorized as clerical was in fact a construction worker, thus the premium collected is incorrect, or false.

Yet another form of fraud consists of a company that decides to change its identification under a newly-formed company name, in order to perhaps extricate itself from a prior negative claim history while simultaneously maintaining low-rate insurance premiums. Other third-party entities that might be involved in fraudulent activities within the Workers' Compensation system can include both insurance agents and claims representatives. For example, insurance agents have been known to collect insurance premium payments and keep the money for themselves leaving the individuals uninsured. Insurance claims adjusters have been caught hiding the results of an Independent Medical Examination in order to settle an injured worker's case for less than full value (169). An insurance claims manager defrauded the company of more than a half-million dollars over a four-year period by issuing claim checks to dummy companies that he endorsed (170) for himself.

OCCUPATIONAL MEDICINE

The majority of those physicians engaged in the practice of Occupational Medicine do so through means of knowledge gained through various forms of self-study, hands-on practical experience, and via attendance of and participation in university-based or other types of short-term coursework (84). Approximately 1,500 physicians possess Board Certification in the specialty practice of Occupational Medicine currently. The Institute of Medicine, with 1,345 members, is a branch of the National Academy of Sciences that is concerned with medical care, research and education and is located in Washington DC and reports to congress, annually. It has put forth the claim that there exists a critical shortage of specialty-trained occupational and environmental physicians (95, 96). A drastic and severe shortage is evident in the network of front-line primary care physicians willing and able to care for patients with occupationally- and environmentally-based illnesses. Despite this scarcity of highly-trained professionals, the specialty continues an increased upward growth pattern in terms of scope of services offered in relation to industrial- and insurer-based demand.

The increasingly complex nature of our society, most of which can be attributed to the rapidity of technological advancement, also adds to the intricacy of workplace environments in the new millennium. In association with these astonishing and explosive changes in the traditional methods for conducting business in our society, we no doubt will continue to experience a burgeoning need and, indeed, a demand for a greater and more knowledgeable body of medically-trained force of professionals to enter into the field of Occupational Medicine. These factors contribute to an increasing need to address the problems that inherently exist in the field of Occupational Medicine as well as newly emerging problems that might be observed as surfacing with further technological and industrial advancements of the future. Work-related injuries and worker-employee relationships all form an integral piece of the business community puzzle that require in-depth understanding in order to formulate innovative and visionary modes for managing these ever-changing systems. The Workers' Compensation system and its foundations support the bridge between the employer and employee to form a cohesive unit to both increase productivity and increase bottom-line revenues, thus benefiting worker and management alike. A comprehensive and thoughtful understanding of this system can only greatly enhance the melding of these two elements of the vast network we call our business and corporate culture.

Chapter Three

The Injured Worker
and the Healthcare Professional

PATIENTS

When working in the field of Occupational Medicine, no matter the capacity, one is often preceded by his or her reputation. In such cases, the medical professional assumes the role of *company doctor*, or physician, as selected by either the employer or insurance company. From the vantage point of the patient, the medical professional comes equipped with predisposed bias, a perception that can often be evidenced in many patients, despite having only recently been initiated into your tenure of employment. Often, the reputation of the clinic has developed over time amongst those workers who have served in some capacity for a lengthy period. These perceptions are often transferred to the incoming newly-hired physician, irrespective of his or her own belief system or code and standard of ethics as a distinct philosophy from that of the clinic. Simply stated, as the physician, you are being judged to be an integral component of the clinic, without benefit of patient knowledge of your own standards of practice that might have been well-established prior to your newly-acquired position in the organization.

Any medical doctor practicing in the field of occupational medicine must adhere to the principles of ethics that dictate an unbiased approach that extends to all patients, the fundaments of which include the fair and equitable treatment of all patients. However, a majority of patients are not necessarily cognizant of this tenet. The very real possibility exists as well that many employers, as well as insurance companies, will view you with at least a modicum of suspicion, fearful of potential bias in favor of the employee.

Further, a certain percentage of patients might misinterpret the content of what you convey to them, the result of which might be the potential for future unfounded complaints filed against you. In some instances, we might view this as a form of patient empowerment, or means by which patients can migrate to alternative medical treatment facilities and providers. The purpose of this shift to competitive treatment facilities acts as a means for patients to enjoy greater degrees of influence in the decision-making process of physicians, with the hoped-for results being favorable patient judgments.

Those engaged in the field of Occupational Medicine often practice medicine that spans a multiplicity of specialty boundaries, requiring a diversity of knowledge bases not often witnessed in most medical fields. As distinct from general practice, Occupational Medicine can at times be an isolating and lonely activity, often lacking the foundation of permanency and more often than not deficient in retaining a solid patient base. This can be viewed as akin to a revolving door, in many respects, with a practitioner of Occupational Medicine often caring for a variety of patients over short time spans, many of whom he or she will likely not encounter again, wholly distinct from the experience of general medical practitioners who often retain patient bases for extended periods of time.

Another area of concern surrounds the expectation level for effective physician performance that, in turn, can be equated with abundant monetary savings for both employer and insurance company alike. Notwithstanding these expectations, scant accolades are forthcoming for the practitioner of Occupational Medicine. Rather, satisfaction and reward are often experienced in more quiet fashion, often gleaned from aiding injured workers toward speedy recovery, the primary focus and objective of which is to remove patients from the system in as hasty a manner as possible. These objectives are maintained by Occupational Medical Practitioners despite many patients displaying a measurable reluctance to terminate their care, for a variety of reasons. Besides taking paid time off from work to return to the clinic, some workers state they are afraid of long term consequences as a result of the injury after being discharged, and some appear to be playing a game with a hidden agenda.

Work is a tangibly important element of any individual's well-being, so much so that the resolution of work-related conflicts and issues is often more significant than is often realized by employees. A majority of injured workers do not necessarily understand the principle that protracted participation in the Workers' Compensation system can pose a psychologically detrimental threat (75) to the employee. Those external to the system might well view skeptically those who are under the aegis of the Workers' Compensation program for extended periods. Often, the authenticity and validity of their injuries might come under questioning, in addition to the possibility that these individuals might be viewed as "milking the system." During periods of delayed recovery, it is not uncommon to frequently evidence workers being mandated to prove the validity of their illnesses by undertaking a complex process of extensive treatment and testing procedures. Additionally, a definitive stigma appears to attach to any individual receiving Workers' Compensation benefits, whether the claim is legitimate or not. Those participating in the system are often perceived to be *manipulators*, perhaps engaging in contrivances for self-gain, and considered highly undeserving of their rewards (79).

It is safe to state that you will not be given congratulatory pats on the back for fiscal savings you have contributed to either the employer or insurance company. Although the beneficiaries of your activities might well appreciate your efforts to some degree, these praises and loyalties might indeed be short-lived. One need consider, then, this very activity to be one for which there exists a high level of expectation to begin with, and acts as explanation as to why meager awards are accorded the medical practitioner in the field of Occupational Medicine. Society too appears contemptuous of the monetary benefits that accrue from this system, most particularly when a system of rationing of medical care is instituted. This might be viewed as a byproduct of what is now termed the consumer movement that exists within the medical industry. This movement works diligently toward instructing patients in methods for developing patient assertiveness, training and guiding patients in strategies that question physician recommendations, and in initiating demands for interventional processes that might otherwise be obstructed. At present, a decided and marked shift has been observed away from the paternalism customarily associated with physician care toward a level of greater patient autonomy. This trend exists and is experiencing record growth despite the concomitant demands it brings with it that often pose a potential detrimental effect to the general social system.

When denying injured worker benefits, it is mandatory for the medical provider to also submit valid explanation for having declined this claim. It is traditionally considered to be unsatisfactory from the vantage point of the employee to include as reason for denial that of unnecessary costs that might accompany the claim. Wastefulness within the system, such as a request for tests and treatment protocols deemed to be unnecessary, or low-cost benefit treatments or regimens, should be avoided if at all possible, due not only to cost-prohibitive factors, but as means to maintain compliance with the tenets of sound medical principles. This forms the rudiments of good medical practice. Unfortunately, the injured worker might be justified in the belief that costs are being maintained at a low level at the expense of his or her well-being. These issues certainly speak to a need for further explanation and understanding in their far-reaching ability to affect all parties involved in the arena of Occupational Medicine.

BACKGROUND

Historically, the traditional doctor-patient relationship has consisted of an informal contract, if you will, between two parties: that of the Healthcare Professional (HCP) and the Patient. "We are actors playing in a theater of social, personality, and cultural systems. The physical environment is the only part that does not interact with us." This statement was asserted one-half century ago by Talcott Parsons (124), the first social scientist to have described this unique relationship. Parsons founded his belief on the assumption that illness derived from a form of dysfunction and rooted itself in social deviance, one requiring a reintegration into the mainstream of social culture. Illness, as well as the act of malingering, provided license for individuals to exempt themselves not only from work-related activity, but other social responsibilities as well. If left unhindered or uncontrolled, these types of behaviors often gave rise to potentially detrimental elements throughout the natural social order. In this regard, the role of illness evolved to become a methodology or means by which to control these deviant behaviors the objective of which was the maintenance of social order. By logical extension, a methodology was formed that envisioned illness as but a transitional stage toward achieving the return to a more normalized or functioning role within the construct of societal and cultural activity, work-related responsibilities to be included as well. In this dynamic, the physician thus assumed the role of overseer, acting as the control mechanism by which to curtail or halt this deviant behavior from that of societal norms. In communicating to the patient, the physician was in a position to advance a set of four social norms governing the functional role of illness, as enumerated below:

1. The individual bears no responsibility for his or her illness.
2. Illness exempts one from normal obligations until recovery is attained.
3. Illness is an undesirable state.
4. The ill should seek professional care.

Having mastered an extensive body of technical knowledge, in accordance with their role expectations, physicians were logically accorded professional autonomy by society as a means for controlling patient illness. As recently as twenty-five years ago, most major medical decisions lay exclusively within the purview of physicians. Although predominantly well-intentioned, these decisions were often reached without benefit of open-ended discussion or public forum, much less the full participation of patients (122). Currently, society has witnessed a measurable shift away from the traditional and more paternalistic approach to medicine, and a trend toward greater patient auton-

omy. Patients are now the predominating force that drives critical medical decisions (123) resulting from a rise in what here is termed "health con-
sumerism." This new philosophical-based trend in medicine both promotes
and encourages the development of greater contractual, albeit conflicting, relationships between patient and physician. Through myriad channels, an
increasingly well-educated populous now challenges medical authority from
a variety of perspectives, relegating the once sacrosanct doctor-patient bond
to that of yet one more provider-consumer interaction, no longer imbued with
the sacred trust that, in order to progress successfully, mandated both compliance and deference.

OTHER PARTIES

Along with the intrusion of other parties into the doctor-patient relationship,
change can often be seen to occur that might negatively interfere with the
achievement of maximum benefit that might otherwise occur. The distinct elements inherent in each individual personality, when commingled with those
of another party often serve to create a third entity or personality, exhibiting
variances in attributes and often contingent upon the chemistry involved. This
phenomenon is often difficult to elucidate or qualitatively identify when one
considers the vast number of variables that determine and comprise our
unique personas, yet it is not impossible to acknowledge the intricacy of relationships that form between patient and doctor ensuing from this fusion of
personalities.

In each incident that one adds another individual to the original equation,
a change takes effect in that resulting interaction. For example, consider the
spouse that accompanies his wife to the doctor. The presence of this third
party in the room creates a diversion in the full attention his wife would otherwise receive, even if her spouse offers nothing in the way of words. One
will immediately notice the change in the way in which his wife behaves, as
distinct from behavior she might have displayed had he not been present. Her
responses and reactions might not be as forthcoming and straightforward
when voicing her complaints; her husband might be found to issue statements
contradictory to that of his wife. As a family member, his needs should me
met as well as that of the wife, thus the physician might find the husband pro-
jecting his own needs as an overlay to his wife's circumstances, precluding
the much-needed attention of the physician to be focused on the patient.

In the same vein, however, the husband might be found to be of the firm belief that he is performing an invaluable service and role in assisting his wife in
recalling recent episodes or events surrounding her illness. He is also proffering

his subjective opinion, based upon and gathered from personal observation. In most instances, in fact, the husband is working to obstruct rather than advance progress. Studies have been conducted that involve individuals suffering from back pain who contact medical professionals in the accompaniment of overly solicitous spouses. In these studies, it has been demonstrated that the spouses often display support by exhibiting overly-accommodating behaviors, the result of which is the ill spouse suffered on average four times the amount of back pain in comparison to those who did not receive such high levels of overzealous support (37).

One can always account for reasons as to why an individual is accompanied by a support person when visiting a medical practitioner. An effort should be made to first address the patient, only involving the companion once patient permission has been given. In spite of this, practitioners of Occupational Medicine often find themselves mired in a dual-member team that includes both patient and support system in the form of a spouse, companion, friend, or others. The practitioner might then find the room contains two patients: one suffering from illness, the other from fear, worry, and/or a hidden agenda. The second individual might be present in order to prevent the truth from emerging, as a means for reinforcing the illness, or to act in the role of coach with future litigation as the objective.

We all impact others to some degree and, when emotional attachment is evident, such as that observed with a relative, friend, or employer, the effect is all that much more profound, with the outcome often being either positive or negative, and oftentimes quite unpredictable. Circumstances such as these will serve as the introduction to the current climate exhibited within the context of the Workers' Compensation system.

THE WORKERS' COMPENSATION SYSTEM

Goals

In providing care to an injured worker, the medical provider must often contend with a multiplicity of other parties also embedded in the system. Let us first examine the existing relationship between medical provider and injured worker. As is the case throughout several States, the employer initially selects the treatment facility for the worker. This alone is sufficient enough reason for suspicions to rise to the surface for the employee as to whose best interests are being served in light of the primary motivations of the medical provider—the employer or the employee? When minor injuries are involved, owing to treatment extending for only short periods of time, the employee is then processed out of the system rather quickly. However, in cases of delayed recovery injuries, accompanied by protracted periods of medical care, this might prove to be a significant factor in the patient's response to treatment modalities.

It is only natural to then assume that the employer and injured worker possess commonly-held goals and attitudes, yet frequently as not their interests prove to be widely divergent. It is not uncommon to evidence a worker seeking respite from a labor-intensive job, while the employer is desirous of the worker continuing to perform the same activities if at all possible. The worker then harbors resentment at having been injured while performing work-related duties that net his employer profits, while the employer is possessed of resentment at the worker having reported an injury, questioning both the validity of this claim, and simultaneously concerned at the potential for this claim to cause an increase in his insurance premiums.

The current medical system as external to that of the Workers' Compensation program operates under the edicts of a patient advocate system. The primary medical provider consists of a family practitioner, catering primarily to the needs of the patient, one that supersedes the interests of other parties (34). This trust- and respect-based relationship has established itself over the course of many years. It is common to witness disappointment, therefore, when patients encounter a situation entirely different as is seen in the practice of Occupational Medicine, operating not as patient advocates per se. Rather, Occupational Medicine practitioners administer medical care within the context of a medical/legal framework, the responsibilities of which are to protect the rights of all interested parties, including not only the employer and injured worker, but the insurance company as well. All parties enjoy specific rights that must be recognized, appreciated, and protected as such. However, this neither places the worker at a disadvantage nor accord him special advantages that he would otherwise possess in a traditionally-based medical care system.

The insurance company, as the controlling financial power, employs an adjuster whose delegated responsibility it is to supervise the care and authorize treatment options, as well as oversee the protection of their interests. The majority of employers seek fair management in a given situation so that the injured worker receives high-quality and appropriate treatment in order that both recovery and resumption of work-related duties are swiftly executed. Employers are often appreciative of the past work and a service performed by their employees and no doubt it serves their best interest that the worker achieves a full and prompt recovery. Obviously, therefore, the use of unscrupulous and unethical health care providers would be considered counterproductive to their employees, potentially resulting in future litigation and possibly causing workers to become disgruntled. Discontented employees can often result in negative outcomes for all parties, not to mention the potential for poor productivity levels and decrease in overall employee morale.

The initial visit presents the opportunity to become acquainted and establish a rapport between medical professional and patient. A detailed history that records the circumstances surrounding the injury's events can prove to be invaluable further on in the process of those litigated cases, thus it is paramount that one establish at the outset a level of control of the case in order to avoid patient manipulation (78, 79). Unless a worker returns to full-scale employment activities, modified duty should be enabled in 95 percent of cases. In theory, modified duty always exists as an option, contingent upon its elective use by the employer. Further details regarding modified duty are discussed in the section below.

Modified Duty

Insurance provisions of the Workers' Compensation system include Modified Duty, defined as being an agreement contractual in nature between the employer and the insurer, falling within the framework of administrative and statutory law, but not within the jurisdiction of Labor Code provisions. It essentially includes the understanding that, as an agreed-upon provision by the employer, the loss of hours worked that would potentially be covered by insurance disability payments will not be required to be paid, the end result of which is a decrease in the assessed estimated risk and which determines insurance premium rates to the employer will be decreased. This option maintains low-cost rates to the employer, and provides medical benefits as well, owing to those injured workers on modified duty recover at a more rapid rate while continuing to participate in the workforce. In psychological terms, they continue to participate in work-related activities in the workplace, remaining as a functioning, integral part of the team, thus enhancing their levels of self-esteem. If unable to work and at home, inactivity ensues, placing undue focus on their illness and, in most cases, becomes a counterproductive element in the recovery process. This option avails the worker the option of temporarily assigned alternative work-related activities as an accommodation to the disability by the employer, an arrangement that measurably benefits both parties.

Should a dispute arise regarding the performance of modified duty, it is imperative that legal resolution be initiated based upon both medically-based opinion and verifiable evidence. The dispute goes to the issue of entitlement of disability benefit payments to the employee. Only one decision need be reached by the worker—that of either accepting or declining the option of a modified duty arrangement, with refusal by the employee resulting in denial of disability payments for lost work hours by the insurer. The Court traditionally upholds this loss of entitlement. A similar situation exists within the sphere of non-work-related medical absences, as in those cases in which an employer demonstrates willingness to provide alternative work activities in accommodation of the employee's temporary impairment that is causing the disability. The worker's refusal to perform such duties will result in loss of their disability insurance benefits owing to the availability of alternative work arrangement options.

Medication

Non-narcotic pain medication is the rule, and should be applied in most industrial injuries. Although several patients might request narcotic pain medication, if granted, it should be administered moderately and only for periods of short duration. Drugs that fall under the classification of Codeine and Hydrocodone are at times seen to cause what is termed the "rebound effect," an outcome that is demonstrated by an increase in pain once the medication's effects wear off, often increasing the pain to a level beyond that originally experienced (101). The initial pleasurable effect is followed by a rebound unpleasant effect because the body's natural endorphins are suppressed by the medication creating a physical demand for the drug, possibly leading to addiction. Amazingly, the very drug to relieve pain becomes the cause of pain. This effect is similar in many respects to the use of a heating pad which, when initially used, demonstrates positive effect, but a rebound effect occurs with continued use causing increased discomfort once the heat element is removed. The cause of this appears to be muscle spasm, which is increased, because the prolongation of the local application of heat has caused injury, in itself. Remember, that we are not dealing with terminal cancer patients in need of pain relief, but self limited minor injuries that should be categorized as so.

Rehabilitation

When at all possible, emphasis should be placed on exercise therapy for rehabilitative treatment of injury, usually termed "Sports Medicine Management." This type of treatment is characterized by active therapy, proven to be beneficial in shortening recovery time. In the alternative, passive therapies, which produce positive responses initially, have demonstrated little if any lasting benefits. Passive physical therapy refers to heat and ice packs, ultrasound, and Manipulation, i.e. things that are done to the patient by the therapist. On the other hand, exercise therapies frequently produce negative responses when initially administered, but serve to provide long-term, lasting benefits to the patient, thus shortening the recovery time, most especially when musculotendinous injuries are involved. Physical therapy might demonstrate more effectiveness if ordered early on in the treatment regimen than later, beginning at the advent of injury. The objective goal of medical treatment interventions is aimed at reactivation of functionality of the injured worker. This also can be viewed as an educational model from which the patient is trained in methods to improve both posture and body mechanics, while increasing overall physical levels of fitness, coordination, and flexibility of motion.

Those engaged in the practice of Occupational Medicine should remain flexible in their ability to compromise in matters concerning treatment strategies; most patients differ in terms of need and personal response to treatment methods. The optimal, ideal method is one in which an individualized treatment strategy is fashioned specifically to suit the given patient, allowing the patient to experience your sensitivity to their particular concerns. It is also quite helpful to communicate with the company representative at this juncture in order to establish corroboration of the injury, employee work status, and to discuss available strategies for medical treatment.

Progress

Follow-up visits are used as a means to determine patient treatment progress, modifications of work schedules and activities, if any, and equally important level of *compliance*. Compliance with medical treatment is believed to be the main determinant of whether success is achieved in the shortest possible time. It is measured by how well the patient adheres with taking their medication, keeping appointments, and following instructions. Measurable gains will be made in this process if you are able to secure a report from the therapist, including levels of medication required and needed, and knowledge of missed or cancelled appointments. Delays in the initiation of physical therapy are not considered uncommon, and might not be through any fault of the patient. Sometimes, there is a delay in approval for payment for therapy by the insurance company, or the therapists are too busy. In some casers, if the patient does not appear to require pain medications, the claimed severity of pain might be considered questionable.

It is of paramount importance to establish both the tone and expediency of therapy, as oftentimes it will be noticed that the injured worker might adopt an attitude similar to that of the treating physician. If the Occupational Medicine professional appears to not require any urgency in recovery for the patient, this will transfer to the patient as well; he or she will also perceive little or no need to hasten the recovery process. When treatment delay does occur, whether resulting from system inefficiencies or questionability of causation, the situation can frequently spiral to an out-of-control stage for the medical treatment provider, in turn leading to excessive costs passed along to the payer.

Those employers who encourage workers to not file claims for injury, attempting to determine if the problem might simply disappear over time, or as means to prevent the addition of insurance surcharges, might cause further problems to develop over a long-term course. Immediate treatment administration is the first step necessary to the achievement of effective case management and its absence is notable in some cases. In those cases in which there has been a noticeable delay in treatment protocol, when finally presented for treatment, those patients falling into this category often demonstrate symptoms that parallel or are collateral to that of sub-acute or chronic stages of injury, thus requiring prolonged treatment regimens in order to reach full-stage recovery. For obvious reasons, the delay of immediate treatment strategies can result in far-reaching negative impacts to both the injured worker and employer alike, most especially considering that state is highly preventable and can be avoided when effective case management techniques are effectively put into operation.

The time spent with the patient involves issues of timeliness, quantity, and quality, thus one cannot emphasize sufficiently the importance of demonstrating respect for each patient, through efforts at promptness and allowance of substantial enough time in which to address all issues and questions that might emerge through interaction with the patient. Being cognizant of and acknowledging the motivations underlying the injured worker's problems and associated illness behaviors will lead to a vastly improved and higher level of effective medical care.

FAMILY MEMBERS

In general, family members usually remain in the waiting room during patient visits, but on occasion are known, through assertive behavior, to accompany patients to the examining room. Rather than exhibiting a confrontational stance, it might serve the Occupational Medicine practitioner to assess the family member as well as the patient, in order to determine the motivations that propelled their behavior. In many instances, it is not unusual to discover that a family member has assumed the role of disability enabler, attempting to coddle the patient. In other words, they have taken it upon themselves to manage both the illness and disability in an indirect manner, as well as serving as coaches for "illness behavior." Often, many individuals who assume this responsibility have played out this routine in the past with other illnesses, as one cannot help but notice their acute levels of skill at performing this role. It serves the provider and patient alike best to confine the appointment to the patient following contact and brief communication with their companion, or significant other, thus maintaining a level track for patient and physician relationship.

SUPERVISOR

Another pitfall to be wary of is that occurring when the patient or injured worker is accompanied by his or her supervisor. In some cases, company policy makes allowance for this policy, despite its violation of the medical code of ethics as well as the Medical Privacy Act. Briefly, the confidentiality of health care information is governed by various federal, state, and local statutes, ordinances, regulations, and case law. The disclosure of personally identifiable health care information can profoundly affect people's lives. "It affects decisions on whether they are hired or fired; whether they can secure business licenses, and life insurance; whether they are permitted to drive cars. . . . (171). In spite of the worker having granted permission for his or her supervisor to be present, there can also exist measurable pressure applied to the patient to comply with the supervisor's request to be present; or, it might otherwise be perceived as an attempt to deceive the employer, as though having something to hide, should the employee refuse the request. In cases involving minor trauma, having a supervisor present while examining the patient will generally not present a problem. However, when dealing with cases of a more medically intricate nature, administration of patient exams should be done without the presence of an employee's supervisor.

CASE MANAGER

At times, the insurance company will assign a case manager to accompany the patient into the examining room, providing the patient has granted permission to do so. A number of case managers are quite adept at removing obstacles to the resolution of medical issues, while others appear to create a preponderance of more problems than existed prior to their involvement. This type of management style can be viewed as an indirect method of applying pressure to the treatment provider as a means to induce a desired change in the course of treatment for a patient that is displaying a delay in or protracted course of recovery time.

PRACTICE GUIDELINES

Guidelines for treatment management are precisely that, not standardized or mandated directives. A large proportion of patients possess symptomatology that does not find resolution in the customary or average length of time generally observed for that given disorder. Delayed recovery is not infrequent in the specialty of Occupational Medicine, and patience is considered a significant prerequisite for successful outcomes. Furthermore, these guidelines can at times act as barriers to appropriate treatment protocols, particularly in those cases in which insurance adjusters religiously adhere to their strictures. This might in fact delay urgent need for authorization of much-needed imaging studies or medical consultation. Some insurance adjusters are simply not professionally equipped to understand the variances and finer nuances of medical practice, and are of the firm belief that they are, rather, dealing with an incompetent practitioner as contrasted to an astute clinician. One can thus imagine the frustration experienced by the treatment provider when one compares the disparity in educational backgrounds between the medical practitioner and insurance adjuster.

DELAYED RECOVERY

Psychosocial issues are the most commonly-noted rationales for delays in recovery time. Roles assumed by other parties might hinder patient recovery, and might include an individual perhaps not even known to the medical provider—a family member who received monetary settlement resulting from an injury or conflict with a workplace supervisor.

It is not infrequent to observe that, upon a patient retaining legal professional, the medical condition often worsens, along with a noted decrease in the patient's ability to return to normal work-related activity until a settlement is reached. One explanation owing to this behavior might lie in the patient having to substantiate the severity of his or her illness to the extent they have claimed. It might well prove counterproductive to their employment situation if their statements should conflict with their originally-stated contentions that they have incurred significantly severe injury requiring legal representation. For example, after someone obtains a lawyer, complete recovery occurs, leaving nothing to litigate. The lawyer is not paid; he or she can only collect their fee from a percentage of the award by law. Complete recovery infers that the injury was not that serious to begin with and thus not in need of legal representation. Why was the lawyer obtained? Was this person exaggerating their injury on purpose for an undeserved benefit? All these questions are avoided by the individual remaining injured.

PATIENT RELATIONS

Defined as "unconsciously applying feelings, attitudes, and expectations from important persons in one's past to people in one's current situation," Transference can occur to some degree in all human relationships. Transference forms the basis for an individual's responses, both emotional and visceral, to other people throughout the course of a lifetime (82). This behavior is observed to develop between patient and physician, and can present in either a positive or negative light.

Positive transference often enhances the healing process, while negative transference, as often evidenced in patients appearing unreasonably suspicious, hostile, litigious, antagonistic, provocative, and excessively dependent, provides useful indicators to the physician of an ensuring problem within the framework of the therapeutic alliance. This alliance is based upon the mutual agreement between patient and physician to work as a cohesive unit of which the objective is attaining an optimal level of benefit to the patient in accordance with treatment strategies.

In general, the medical provider exhibiting an attitude of concern, respect, honesty, and courtesy, in combination with both empathic responses and protection of issues surrounding privacy and confidentiality, can work cohesively to foster a positive relationship between physician and patient. We have learned that improved communication and communication strategies used in the doctor and patient relationship will add measurably to mutually-beneficial satisfaction, more positive clinical outcomes for patients, a decrease in the rate of malpractice lawsuits, and will enable the practitioner to perform in a more thorough and capable manner without also increasing the time allotted to each patient.

The primary focus of medical education is that of curing disease via methods utilizing either drug therapy or surgical procedure, or a combination of both, more so than healing illness per se, which requires at times appropriate use of language, manner and tenor of physician demeanor, and personalized responses to the emotional base of the patient (83). We would do well to remember that disease is the pathological entity, while illness, in contrast, is the means by which an individual *perceives* that disease. The patient who presents with a positive attitude can be classified as possessing a minimal or minor illness, despite also presenting with a major disease, and the converse holds true as well. "It is clear that disease and illness are not the same. Many patients may have "silent" disease where some physiological disruption, that they are not aware of, is present. Similarly, there are many people who have illnesses but have no evidence of physiological disease. The behaviors of persons may vary greatly according to whether or not they perceive themselves as ill (82)."

BASIC INTERVIEW

A *social history* should be recorded first, rather than the primary complaint and illness, as we were originally taught. Allow the patient to voice their opinions and complaints for one full minute without interruption, while sitting closely at eye level with the patient. Make noticeable eye contact with the patient, not the chart. It can be refreshingly therapeutic for the patient to be afforded the time necessary to recount his or her story, and will fuse the connection between patient and physician. The most reliable predictor of patient compliance is the patient's sense of the level of attention being paid to his or her medical issues. In the final analysis, the doctor and patient will hopefully have forged a jointly-constructed task that includes completing the history of the illness as agreed-upon by both parties (83). The forging of a partnership or marriage of both patient and doctor with commonly-held goals and objectives for treatment protocols, once an agreed-upon determination has been reached regarding the presenting injury and related illness, will sizably improve the chances of rapid patient recovery.

Within the context and process of working in joint partnership to formulate the history of the illness will aid the doctor and patient alike to then agree upon options for treatment. In paraphrasing that which the patient has communicated, the physician will elicit an improved understanding of the patient by demonstrating trust in and validation of the patient's concerns. The art of paraphrasing works as well as a form of summarization of the patient's recounting of his or her injury and associated illness, allowing for the patient to hear once again those elements that comprise the injury and move the process forward to now deal with treatment concerns. This process can be viewed as the primary tool used to communicate empathy for the patient, serving as an extremely useful therapeutic device.

Non-verbal communication, or body language and cues, can be considered more powerfully evocative than verbal communication (89). Furthermore, it has been observed that the manner and tone in which something is communicated is equally as important as the content of the communication itself (98). Ineffectual and inaccurate listening mechanisms and abilities can often lead to diagnostic and therapeutic errors, further helping to convince the patient of physician incompetence.

Doctors and patients are often seen to assign blame to one another in cases in which interaction has reached a level of dysfunction, no longer effective in the treatment process. This scenario can occur when either one or both parties perceive a successful outcome to be improbable, where expectations are neither parallel to each other or misaligned, or in cases where there is evidence of blatant inflexibility of the part of either party. These types of difficulties that are recognized early on in the treatment process, in order to ascertain whether the disruption has been caused by patient affect, such as anger, sadness, fear, or a syndrome based in psychosocial issues, can greatly hasten the positive resolution of the problem. If the problem has been determined to be the case, i.e., the patient is displaying negative affect; address that problem directly as the first order of business. Alternatively, if the problem does not appear to originate from the patient, attempts should be made to share the problem perceived by you with the patient, requesting his or her input and partnership in resolving the issue.

At times, doctor and patient fail to reach agreement on either the diagnosis itself or course of treatment to be followed. In such cases, the patient invariably exhibits refusal or reluctance to abide by physician instructions. Several possible solutions to this dilemma might include the following:

1. If there exists a major disparity between the theory posited by the physician and that of the patient, the issues should be jointly examined.
2. Opening up the disagreement for discussion will begin the process of negotiation.
3. Lend support and weight to the opinion of the patient as an act of respect.
4. During discussion, practice empathic communication techniques. Rephrasing of patient's thoughts and concerns, and then repeating back to the patient a summary of his or her statements, will act as acknowledgment of your understanding of his or her words and meanings, decreasing the possibility for misinterpretation or miscommunication.
5. Should efforts at negotiation fail, the patient and physician can simply agree to disagree, amicably terminating the relationship without further conflict or confrontation.

Physician effectiveness cannot be accomplished in an atmosphere of patient anger or hostility. Once this hostility or resentment is recognized, it will serve us well to modestly retreat and reflect on the events and interactions, then proceed to discuss with the patient the probable causes of conflict. The problem might well find remediation through the use of empathic response mechanisms. In order to increase patient compliance, understanding the patient's perspective of what constitutes the illness, its underlying causes, and appropriate treatment regimen are paramount elements. Several factors that might result in noncompliance are as follows:

• Failure of the physician to explain and further elaborate the illness and medical ramifications and treatment regimen.
• Failure of the patient to fully understand physician's explanation.
• Failure on the part of the patient to comprehend written materials associated with illness and/or treatment modalities.
• Monetary costs of treatment associated with time, as well as framework for recovery time, comfort, and effort needed to hasten progress.

- Patient concerns voiced regarding side-effects of treatment.
- Conflict resulting from disparity between patient and physician concepts regarding nature of illness and therapeutic regimes.
- Patient inability to recall elements of physician instructions.

RETURN TO WORK

The return-to-work process is facilitated by two important elements, the first grounded in obtaining the most effective medical care as promptly as possible, and the reduction of emotional stress that potentially follows an injury. In order to assist in receiving them most prompt medical treatment, several insurers are aiding the process by assisting employers in filing a "first notice of injury" with the appropriate State agency responsible for oversight of the Workers' Compensation system. This step assists greatly in driving the claim process forward. In addition, these insurers encourage improved communications between employer and employee in regard to the Workers' Compensation system in advance of and as a preemptive measure prior to injury occurrence. An individual equipped with knowledge of what to expect and who is eligible to receive medical attention promptly will also demonstrate more speedy recuperation times, while being less likely to turn to legal representation for assistance. The second aspect of this dynamic is that, once injured workers are removed from their normal work-related activities, in order that they remain an integral member of the workplace team, the employer should maintain regularized contact with the employee on a frequent basis.

Extended absences from work can often result in producing a lasting negative impact on a worker's future employment opportunities and economic stability. Medical providers are often found to both create and define expectations surrounding recovery issues. In many respects, it is a daunting responsibility, and one for which a good many doctors themselves might be unaware.

SYSTEM

Workers' Compensation systems possess voluminous databases from which to undertake outcome evaluations of their own processes, however little if any data are made available or accessible to the general public. For example, the National Council on Compensation Insurance (NCCI) collects, processes, and analyzes data from private workers' compensation insurance on up to 50% of claims and policies in the United States. It helps insurance companies to

determine rates and government agencies for data concerning legislation
(172). These systems are not often equipped or designed to provide such high
levels of information to the average consumer. Long term follow up of individual patients are not possible because of the Medical Privacy Acts. Insurance schemata are often observed to have paid and continue to pay for healthcare services based, in part, on an innate fear of antagonizing health
professionals unless fraud can be proven. Because of these obstructions, little
or no research has been conducted based on the effects resulting from varied
compensation arrangements or interactions with healthcare facilities and patient outcomes.

Throughout the Workers' Compensation industry, the use of information
technology remains in a state of nascency. From the vantage point of the Internet and e-commerce, the insurance industry might well be considered extremely archaic in comparison to other, more advanced social arenas. The
preponderance of data that is required to be downloaded is not immediately
available to the user.

Several of the more specific on-line requisites and ideal desired needs as
requested by risk managers across the nation include:

- Custom-tailored information regarding loss experience, industry trends,
  and comparisons.
- Rapid policy issuance.
- Standardization of software design for claims administration.
- The ability to review information online and in an immediately communi-
  cable fashion, rather than via telephone contact.
- A website serving as a portal for data to include a wide spectrum of risk
  management issues.
- Use of disability duration guidelines by the employer, provider, and claims
  payer.
- Ability for medical providers, claims administrators, safety professionals,
  nursing case managers, and employers to gain access to online communication on a case-specific basis.

One key benefit accrued from the Internet is its unique ability to shorten
the time framework necessary for effective decision-making.

STRESS OF INJURY

One stark challenge facing health professionals and compensation administrators alike is simplifying the workers' compensation system to reduce stress

on the injured worker. At times, the lack of an established correlation between the ostensible gravity of the injury and duration of leave from work, leads to suspicion and mistrust amongst participants in the system. Witnesses to the injury may state that they thought the injury was trivial or that the worker didn't appear hurt. This in turn leads to the adoption of defensive behaviors by the injured party. This may lead to chronic pain to reinforce the validity of the claim. The issue associated with long-term residual pain deriving from seemingly minor injuries requires more in-depth examination to determine whether the same types of behaviors can be attributable to non-compensable injuries as well, or whether they form as part of the "compensation-induced" consequences.

Evidence exists to indicate that employees with non-compensable injuries return to work at a more rapid pace in some situations than those incurring compensable injuries. However, no studies have yet been conducted to determine whether these individuals do so prior to their being, in fact, fit to return to work, or whether any long-term consequences ensue from a rapid return to normalized daily activities.

Because Workers' Compensation systems are not consumer-oriented in nature, they can often appear to act to promote disempowerment of the injured worker. The palpably low degree of data that is provided to the public as well as the perceptions of some percentage of workers receiving Workers' Compensation benefits that they are no longer in control of their lives, contribute to a litany of commonly-held concerns regarding the system. A more profound understanding of the current climate associated with Workers' Compensation is needed in order that a systematized strategy might be designed and developed with the objective and intent of providing sufficient financial and medical care security, acting in the best interests of those we are attempting to assist, rather than as counterproductive to those goals. To that end, the California Department of Industrial Relations introduced a "worker's portal" on the internet on March 4, 2003 to provide information and assistance. Other suggestions are in Chapter 11.

DISABILITY

Independent Medical Examiners are frequently called upon to provide medical opinions that involve disability assessments. These examiners neither assume the role of treatment provider, nor do they perform in the capacity or context of the traditional doctor-patient relationship (86). Rather, the function they serve is that of proffering clinically-based opinion grounded in the history, examination, and appraisal of the patient's impairments. The responsibility of gatekeeper is delegated to the physician, while the claimant is placed in the position of convincing the examining doctor that his or her symptoms are of sufficient enough gravity to warrant passage through the gate.

Involvement in the disability process of determination can direct both the physician and patient alike through unfamiliar territory, in which diagnosis and treatment are oftentimes obscured by non-medical-based factors, such as those including economic, psychosocial, and functional elements. The treatment physician might adopt the role of patient advocate thus, in turn, prejudicing the objectivity of the medical-legal decision-making process. The physician is more accustomed to administering to patients on an independent basis without external interference in his decisions and the decision-making process.

Disability medicine is subsumed within a much larger system, one that includes more individuals and factors than that of the treating physician-patient-illness triumvirate only. The practice of disability medicine also encompasses a legal process within the frame of the administrative sphere. The physician thus acts as one of several professionals ensconced within a domain of greater depth and breadth, to include the patient, the illness or injury itself, the ability for the employee to function in society, and the allocation of distribution of funds. The physician's role amidst this expansive network is relegated to estimating a patient's impairment based on objective assessment. Independent medical assessors are required to possess unbiased evaluative ability and provide a balanced and independently-assessed opinion, and thus are considered to be the preferable assessor of choice.

Inconsistencies can at times stem from the calculation of settlement costs for an injured worker's residual impairment (102). A residual impairment is defined as a permanent loss or abnormality of cognitive, emotional, physiological, or anatomical structure or function after maximum medical improvement (90). One major problem is illustrated in California, whereby a single hypothetical case was disseminated to 65 independent Medical Examiners, all possessing experience in the performance of ratings. Following their having been supplied with the records ascribed to the specific case, a request was made to these physicians to provide estimates of the level of disability based upon their examinations. The degree of disability as calculated by the examiners resulted in respective discrepancies by as much as 85% (103), and the wide variability in calculations resulted in a major source of dispute. The outcomes of this study have led to questions as to the efficacy of the current system employed by practitioners, in areas concerning range-of-motion measurements, and whether in fact it is a valid methodology for determining disability levels.

Additionally, a number of studies demonstrate low rates of correlation between the AMA (American Medical Association) Guides to Permanent Impairment spinal range-of-motion and impairment to patients observed with chronic lower-back pain (104, 105, 106). The spinal range-of-motion is contingent upon the age and gender of the patient (107, 108), degree of osteoarthritis, and the recorded time of day (109), with a low rate of correlation to disability (110). Other studies demonstrate a lack of relationship observed between impairment rating and true residual physical function (111, 112).

CHRONIC PAIN

One of the most formidable challenges facing the Workers' Compensation system involves the evaluation, treatment, and permanent disability rating applicable to those injured workers presenting with chronic pain issues. Many patients exhibiting chronic pain problems maintain normal functional and working-related activities, while other injured workers with chronic pain remain dysfunctional and experience some percentage of unemployment.

Chronic pain is a commonly-shared problem and is variously defined as contingent upon the situation causing difficulty in diagnosis and can often be a frustrating and perplexing syndrome to treat. Suffering the discomfort of chronic pain can be construed as a personalized subjective experience that can often not be either adequately measured or quantified, with evaluation occurring most often only through empirical observation of a patient's behavioral responses to treatment modalities. Chronic pain might have as its root cause a genuinely physical source, one that might emerge in both a subtle and progressive manner, and ultimately take on the characteristics of a disease. Many patients contact multiple specialists and undergo a dizzying array of testing procedures and exams to discover and determine the cause of and subsequent treatment strategy that will advance the healing process. The physician, insurer, employer, and attorney alike experience both frustration and often-healthy skepticism and suspicion surrounding the motivational elements that might underlie the patient's behavior.

Present-day pain management clinics no longer treat a myriad of isolated symptoms often observed in chronic pain patients. Rather, the clinic invokes a more holistic approach to pain management and relief, treating the entire surrounding environmental elements of the patient—that of the body, family relationships, work-related issues, and cultural and psychological disorders. Two complementary assumptions are implicit in this circumstance—that of pain affecting not only the physical functions of the patient, but also impacting all other areas of a patient's existence. As a result, this mode of treatment places considerable focus on multivariate areas. A given patient complaining of back pain who is unable to conduct normal work-related activities is more than likely to experience anxiety and depression as ancillary elements of the discomfort. His or her family relationships will evidence decline as well. The second assumption can be yet more significant in its supposition that the suffering experienced by the chronic pain patient is comprised to a large degree by a combination of emotional, social, professional, and ideological elements. The back pain consists of a higher degree of discomfort due to family relationships having been disrupted as well as chronic pain suffers no longer perceiving themselves to be productive members of society. Pain is both caused and magnified by factors involving depression, isolation, lack of productivity, and disruption of well-being. Much of what is called "the pain of the patient" is, in fact, a form of multi-layered suffering.

Both researchers in the field of pain-related issues and many patients alike are well aware that the possibility exists to be conscious of the sensation of pain, to have knowledge of its existence, yet to not really care. This behavior has frequently been observed in athletes. George (Sparky Anderson), the former Manager of the Detroit Tigers baseball team, once stated to an injured player, "Pain don't hurt." This statement infers the use of mental "dissociation," which often produces a similar effect on intense pain as that of drug therapy, such as morphine, or in situations where hypnosis is the treatment of choice.

The research indicates that pain is not merely localized in the physical body, but also represents a disruption to a more far-reaching intangible area, such as family, community, culture, religion, and that the patient is never a figure in isolation. The patient is in fact an integrated element of a much wider network of animate and inanimate elements that go into the ingredients of a culture or society. When perceived as a form of punishment, pain can work as a means to relieve feelings of guilt, thereby allowing the patient to endure much greater degrees of discomfort. Pain can thus be viewed as a kind of medicinal salve (associated with guilt), a testing ground (boot camp), a rite of passage (fraternity initiation rites), or an aversive physical force (tissue injury) (87).

Averages of nearly 100 percent of patients with chronic pain who have been engaged in treatment programs suffer significant levels of sleep deprivation. This might range from two to three hours of lost sleep per night, or might take the form of what is termed non-restorative sleep. Non-restorative sleep is defined as not achieving enough deep sleep (stages 3 and 4) even though the length of time sleeping may seem adequate. Chronic pain typically impairs the state of deep sleep (Stages 3 and 4), speculated to be a critical factor in the rehabilitative process. Sleep encompasses the foundation underlying the quality of performance and strength as means by which to endure the demands placed on the physical and emotional body. Normal sleep, exercise, and general activity are foundational requisites to feeling normal. In the rehabilitative process, physical activity most generally precedes feeling normal (113, 114). Studies have demonstrated that sleep-deprived subjects possess more irritable, volatile, and depressive tendencies than those of the control groups. Therefore, normal sleep levels should be a prime objective in the design of treatment modalities for chronic pain patients.

The selection process concerned with which patients to treat who are predisposed to chronic pain ailments and in what setting are critical elements and must be executed with care. Treatment should be offered only to those patients who exhibit and present with the most reasonable probability for significant improvement in their conditions. Factors used to determine which patients to exclude from treatment within the framework of a chronic pain program might include the following instructive guidelines:

- Those patients who exhibit inability to understand and carry out instructions.
- Aggressive or violent behavioral tendencies exhibited by patients.
- Suicidal tendencies exhibited by patients.
- Lack of cooperation or unwillingness or reluctance to participate in any elements of the treatment and pain program on the part of the patient.

The optimal methods for physical and occupational therapy should include active exercise, along with limited passive modalities. The goal of intervention is that of functional restoration, a far more cost-effective treatment strategy than traditionally-based passive therapeutic measures, which are, focused more on relief of pain than on increased overall functionality. Chronic pain programs that have as their emphasis the use of narcotics and procedures, such as the administration of nerve blocks, might well be effective in providing temporary beneficial effects, but failure to achieve an increase in overall functional capability and self-sufficiency will render the patient unlikely to maintain any long-term pain subsidence or improvement. The treating physician can best serve the chronic pain patient with reassurance through the use of encouragement and in support of remaining active while continuing to perform work-related activity when at all possible. Any de-emphasis on medications, procedures, therapy, and/or somatic preoccupation will play a significant role in restoring the mental and physical functioning capabilities of chronic pain patients.

THEORY

Syndenham (1624-1689), known as "The English Hippocrates," was instrumental in instituting a major change in the practice of medicine (126). Rather than treating the individual symptoms of the patient in a distinct manner, he advocated the search for and treatment of those underlying causes of the symptomatology (or disease), with the successful outcome of the symptoms either subsiding or being eliminated. In many instances, one is misled by the historical record of a given injury, often pursuing a course of treatment that has little relationship to or association with the patient's current illness. The original injury that initially instigated the process, is now long-healed, despite the patient continuing to present with issues of a symptomatic nature. At what point does an injured worker with a given problem become identified as a patient with an illness? In recognizing that the actual injury itself might only be partially responsible for the injured worker's complaints might be the first significant step toward preventing what is termed iatrogenic-related illness, which in turn can incur unnecessary and cost-intensive testing procedures. Iatrogenic disability is defined as one resulting, in part, from the physician's activity, manner, or therapeutic measures, and not deriving solely from the originally presenting medical condition.

It is in the best interests of the patient that medical care be directed toward the injured worker assuming responsibility for his own health, rehabilitation, and well-being. The health care practitioner should optimally serve as both teacher and guide if this endeavor is to produce successful outcomes. Not unless and until the patient is well-educated in the available diagnosis methodologies and treatment regimens will he or she become an active participation in rehabilitative efforts. Passivity, conversely, can be equated with a personal lack of responsibility for improved functionality and return to a normal level of work-related activity. As is the case in so many intricate areas of human existence, participation in one's own processes for development, whether it be physical, mental, or emotional, should be considered the maximal approach for achieving and maintaining physical health, most especially in the area of rehabilitative procedures. Thus, the Occupational Medical practitioner should use this proviso as a principal element in the guidelines for the practice of sound medicine; the patient's full and undivided focus should be emphasized whenever possible throughout the rehabilitative process as a means by which to instill a higher and more beneficial level of participation. Full-scale patient participation in the healing process will engender patient inspiration, enhancing and fueling the primary objective to return the employee to a status encompassing a more fully functional and normalized work-related level of activity.

Chapter Four

The Injured Worker and Other Stakeholders

An injury is much sooner forgotten than an insult.

—Lord Chesterfield, 1746

The following lists the Stakeholders, or those holding a vested interest, in the Workers' Compensation Program:

Employer	Independent Medical Examiner
Work Supervisor	Certified Language Interpreter
Work Safety Officer	Orthotic Supplier
Insurance Company	Insurance Investigator
Insurance Adjuster	State Legislature
Case Manager	Diagnostic Laboratory Pathologist
Healthcare Professional	Federal Agencies (DOT), if applicable
Hospital	Union
Medical Specialist Consultant	Coworkers
Physical Therapist	Family
Occupational Therapist	Lawyer
Diagnostic Radiologist	Pharmacist
Medical Review Officer	

Although the general stakeholder list is lengthy, the principal stakeholders comprise only the injured worker, employer, the insurance company, and the healthcare provider, with entire industries growing and developing as branches of the Workers' Compensation program, contingent upon whether their orientation is in promoting the rights of either the Worker or the Employer. The primary employer-oriented group comprises the Occupational

Medical Clinic, and the Insurance Company and its legal representatives, while the worker-oriented group is initially constituted by the Occupational Medical Clinic and Insurance Company but, as the claims process enters into a more protracted phase, the composition of this group extends to the Lawyer, secondary health professionals, and the specific Union for which the worker holds membership.

Needless to say, although created as a means to avoid conflict and potential litigation, the system is far removed from being emblematic of that reality. The No-Fault concept and principles adhering to it are often difficult for some workers to embrace, thus they pursue what might be termed a pseudo-litigious course, a self-serving process for the very industry in support of its use. In order to protect his or her rights, an injured worker is informed that legal representation is necessary, based upon the contention that the other providers serve at the favor of the employer. The worker is then referred to a litigant-supportive medical provider, functioning as the medical care delivery system provider over a protracted period of time, culminating at the Workers' Compensation Appeals Board (Court), in opposition to the Insurance Company. The judges, or referees, more frequently than not rule in favor of the worker in support of the laws originally established to protect the rights of the employee. This then serves to explain the means by which 20 percent of these claims are capable of generating 80 percent of the costs associated with the Workers' Compensation system.

The Occupational Medical Provider is mandated to exercise equal treatment of all participants, acting to both respect and protect the rights of all parties involved. This situation induces conflicts and becomes exacerbated, however, because some participants would prefer not being party to the equal treatment tenet; rather, they much more desire favorable or advantaged treatment above the needs and wants of other participants. The legal establishment and union alike are particularly wary and distrustful of employer-appointed medical providers, the sentiments of which are, in turn, conveyed as pertinent information to the worker.

Operating as a medical provider within the system just described, it becomes of singular importance to possess the proper orientation to its various related activities. Barring a miraculous occurrence, symptoms of the work-related injured worker are not likely to resolve unless and until the case has been adjudicated. If the union contributed to the worker's suspicious perspective of the medical provider, there is little if any likelihood that the problem will find resolution without a worker-requested MRI; the same principle holding true for the services of a Medical Consultant. This process is most often utilized as a method for double-checking the conclusions reached by the medical provider, founded upon the belief system of the worker that views the provider with skepticism.

Contrasted to non-work-related problems, the Workers' Compensation System is responsible for generating lengthier treatment periods, higher-dose levels of medication, lengthier physical therapy regimes, and a greater number of diagnostic studies and testing procedures, resulting in more negative outcomes (41, 42, 43, 44, 45, 46, 47). As compared to group health care costs for the same diagnosis and/or service, those cases managed by Workers' Compensation programs are estimated to range from 130 percent to 200% higher, with no ceiling or limitations placed on the costs of treatment. The law clearly states that the injured employee should be treated until the maximum level of medical improvement possible has been achieved. Furthermore, should the condition worsen following a period of stabilization, allowance is made for the case to be reopened within five years from the date of original injury.

The original intent and design of the system was that of ensuring that proper treatment be administered to the injured worker. Unfortunately, a concomitant drawback to the originally created, albeit well-intentioned, system is the development and evolution of marked abuses embedded in the management of the program. Systemic abuses often lead to higher costs and premium rates, translating into higher-priced goods and services for all those engaged in a workplace environment—that is, adversely impacting the majority of the American populace.

Third-party entities, such as the legal agonists and unions, act as only one contributory factor in the growth of medical benefit costs. The State legislatures have been seen to periodically enact legislation that shifts the advantages benefiting one party to that of another, much like a pendulum as it swings back and forth throughout different stages of its movement. It is not unusual to experience one stage of this process in favor of the worker, while at other times the advantage will be focused on the employer. For example, in California in 1989, numerous reforms were passed to encourage parties to avoid litigation and conserve the limited resources of the Workers' Compensation Appeals Board. However, the basis for the award of permanent partial disability benefits—residual impairment—caused an increase in litigation instead (174). The 1989 and 1993 statutory reforms reduced medical-legal payments, but caused a tremendous increase in medical lien filings requiring a special court to handle the increased caseload. The California Workers' Compensation Reform Act of 1993 helped employers by curtailing claims by employees and establishing an 'Employer Bill of Rights". In 2002, AB 749 was passed, favoring the workers, becoming a new law that raised Workers' Compensation for injured workers and penalties increased on employers who fail to obtain workers' compensation insurance (175).

STATISTICS

With a recorded 16.2 million workers in the State of California in 2000, there were 787, 953 recorded workplace injuries and illnesses that year (186,187). Two-thirds of the State employers purchase insurance to cover Workers' Compensation liability, while one-third of the largest employers pay the costs themselves (173).

Forty insurance companies in 1995 retained 96 percent of Workers' Compensation business in the State of California. With 20.8 percent of the market share in 1995, the State Compensation Insurance Fund continues to be the largest insurer. Originally established by the State, this fund currently exists as an independent nonprofit enterprise. In 2003, with a large exodus of insurance companies from California, State Compensation Insurance Fund now has 43 per cent of the market, said Nanci Kramer, deputy press secretary for the state Department of Insurance (180). Nationwide, in the 21 states with state fund models, the state funds now account for 30 per cent in premium written and have a supply motive rather than a profit motive. In the current environment, other states may adopt state funds further altering the competitive situation in this important line of business (189).

On average, one out of every five Workers' Compensation cases results in litigation, with each worker and employer respectively represented by an attorney. There are approximately 1000 attorneys in the State of California whose practices are specialized in the representation of injured workers.

In 2000 a total of $8.9 billion was paid for workers' compensation by California private insurers, self-insured employers, and state funds (188).

The State employees of the California Division of Workers' Compensation are responsible for the management of litigated cases, offering expert opinions on the extent of a given worker's permanent disability, performing reviews of vocational rehabilitation plans, and responding to questions that arise from both workers and auditor claims. State counselors are delegated the management of approximately 800,000 new claims per year, and the responsibility of responding to questions and concerns pertaining to workers.

MANAGED CARE

In the State of Florida in 1993, the legislature mandated that medical care be provided to all employees under the auspices of a managed care model, the objective of which was the reduction of medical care costs while simultaneously maintaining high-quality levels of care. Appointed by the Governor and approved by the legislature, the Florida Task Force on Workers' Compensation Administration recently stated:

> *The intended cost savings that managed care was to bring to the worker compensation system has not been documented by most employers. Instead, mandatory managed care provisions seem to have actually increased medical costs, mostly due to increased administrative expenses. Florida showed the highest use of medical cost containment strategies to seven other states (CT, TX, GA, MA, MN, PA, CA) for which they were benchmarked. . . . Of the seven states surveyed, Florida was the only state that mandated managed care (for all employers).*

The Task Force went on to further state that *litigation* had shown an *increase* based upon several regulations as set forth in the managed care program, pointing out that "employers may still want to have a place in a managed care system, but only if they determine that it is the most effective system for them."

Effective October 1, 2001, the Managed Care provision of the law was repealed by the Florida legislature, with managed care now considered to be optional for employers throughout Florida. A majority of the larger employers in Florida continue to retain various forms of managed care, having recognized the benefits of this program and its ability to reduce the burden of unnecessary administrative expenses.

Based upon and benefiting from Florida's experience with mandated managed care, stakeholders might wish to place more focus on the management of Workers' Compensation programs, utilizing those methods that have proven to reduce costs while optimizing positive outcomes. It is highly unlikely, however, that State legislatures will view managed care as the singular panacea for managing the current financial problems associated with Workers' Compensation presently.

It would appear both prudent and advisable that we shift focus away from viewing managed care as an isolated and all-encompassing solution; rather, attention should be trained on integrating the core components of a given system that prove to be most cost-effective while providing high-quality medical care delivery systems. Both the appropriate use of outcome data and the identification of the actual elements that drive total costs are necessary measures. Payers should concentrate most heavily on those factors that drive costs on a state-by-state and industry-specific basis. Medical benefits for treatments, drugs, and physical therapy, paid by physicians, will vary considerably from one state to another. Through the careful analysis of actual payout founded on category and calculated on a state-by-state basis, a more accurate breakdown of monetary expenditures and use will be provided. Being equipped with a cadre of knowledge regarding outcomes and the elements that drive costs will enable the payer to better formulate strategic claims management programs customized specifically to each distinct region.

INSURANCE INVESTIGATORS

The primary tool used by the insurance companies for fraud detection is that of insurance investigators. A decision need be rendered by the insurer as to whether the cost of investigating a suspect claim can be justified in those cases for which a settlement might produce significantly lower costs than the costs associated with investigation. In many instances, the decision to facilitate a settlement is often chosen as the best means to cut losses and costs.

Those claims that involve settlements below $20,000 are frequently unchallenged. In a large portion of these cases, actual accidents are in fact involved; however, the claims of injury and treatment associated with these accidents are often embellished, revealing acts of fraudulence on the part of those filing the claim.

All United States investigators perform their work under the auspices of the State Open Records Act, based in the specific state in which the investigation is conducted, the Federal Freedom of Information Act (1967, 1975, 2002), and the Federal Privacy Act (1974). These laws, while protecting private confidential information, allow official reports to be made available to the general public, like police reports, OSHA reports, motor vehicle reports, etc.

An effective investigative tool is that of videotape surveillance, the goal of which is to disprove the disability as claimed. This can generally be undertaken by demonstrating that the claimant has engaged in the performance of activities that the worker denied having the ability to execute.

The individual assigned the responsibility of conducting the surveillance and videotaping is considered to be part of the company, thus care must be taken to avoid any harassment of the subject under investigation and that might cause the subject to feel a sense of threat or undue disruption to the claimant's life (68). Although videotape might in fact disclose evidence contradictory to the claimant's alleged disability, the methods used might also have the effect of evoking sympathy for the claimant if it can be demonstrated that he or she was subjected to undue distress through the use of surveillance techniques.

When surveillance is conducted, in many cases, the claimant asserts that he or she had been subjected to harassment and violation of privacy. In order to avoid these types of allegations, strict rules have been established as means to deter illegalities. Traditionally, surveillance will be conducted over a period ranging from two to four hours; with certain activities allowing for lengthier periods should specific activities be observed. Surveillance should occur several times over the course of days or weeks, with continual surveillance on a day-to-day basis to be avoided.

As example, one surveillance videotape revealed a subject relying on the use of crutches as he walked into his physician's office, observed to be in great distress caused by this activity. Another videotape of this same individual leaving the physician's office demonstrated the subject as he tossed the crutches into the rear of his vehicle, jauntily circling his truck and climbing up to a high-level step-up into the driver's seat, observed to do so without difficulty. This incident cast reasonable doubt on the subject's prior observed activity, in which he maneuvered from vehicle to physician's office with apparent stress, but left with none when he thought he was unobserved (68).

It is paramount that surveillance be conducted in full public view, with avoidance of nighttime surveillance. No intrusive activities should be enacted on the claimant's property or the potential exists for it to be construed as a form of trespassing. No forms of entrapment may be employed, such as causing a flat tire to the claimant's vehicle in order to ascertain whether he or she might engage in changing the tire. The individual conducting the surveillance should neither engage in personal contact nor other modes of communication with the subject.

In order that videotaping, which is considered to be a costly endeavor, be considered creditable, it must act not only as a current record of events, but as an ongoing journal of the claimant's activities as well. One isolated act might not be considered sufficiently conclusive enough evidence, thus a series of recorded incidents will act more convincingly to demonstrate the claimant's regular engagement in observable activities.

In that claims investigation is so costly an undertaking, and intricate in its execution, one might easily conclude claims settlement to be the far easier and less exorbitant strategy in which to engage. Nonetheless, this would serve only to further encourage other fraudulent claims activity, negatively impacting all parties in the Workers' Compensation system through the resulting increases in insurance costs, a decision that must be heavily weighed by the insurer.

INSURANCE

Currently, the majority of insurance companies far prefer the use of the term "occurrence," rather than "accident," in which occurrence indicates an incident most likely resulting in a claim for damages covered by an insurance policy. Two obligations must be satisfied by an insurance policy—defense and indemnification. The insurance carrier is ascribed the responsibility to defend the insured against a given claimant's allegations, while the duty to indemnify holds the carrier responsible for payment of a claim on the insured's behalf.

The obligation to defend the insured party is continues to be maintained by the insurance carrier even in those cases that appear to have no basis in merit nor does it bear any relationship to the factual evidence of the case.

The duty to indemnify rests upon either the judgment of the court or stipulations contained in the settlement, with the facts of the allegations bearing upon the outcome.

RETURN TO WORK

Return-to-work issues differ for each participant of a given claims case. The employee's issues might include discontent with the job, one's coworkers, or an immediate supervisor. The employee might exhibit fearful behavior surrounding the issue of re-injury or overt demonstration of a desire to participate in a program of retraining and/or vocational rehabilitation.

Employer and coworker issues involving the worker's return-to-work cannot be overemphasized in importance. In those cases in which the employer demonstrates a reluctance to rehire the individual, or when coworkers are vocally critical of the employee's status under the rubric of modified duty, the injured worker might often experience a sense of being demeaned and unwanted, all serving to encourage an environment fraught with conflict.

It is of utmost importance to formulate a realistic strategy or formalized plan for vocational rehabilitation activities should the worker be ill-equipped to return to a normal level of work-related activity. On a functional level, vocational rehabilitation is an uncertain proposition at best. The individual's abilities and goals are primary considerations and, if beset by poor planning and management, can lead to squandered resources and a decreased perception of self-worth, in addition to increased levels of disability. Obstacles for rehabilitation may reside with the injured worker. Lack of education, particularly illiteracy, is a formidable obstacle in teaching a new skill like TV repair or welding. There is a strong inverse relationship between level of education and work disability among people 25-64 years old (182). According to the Current Population Survey (CPS) 1998, people with less than 8 years of schooling had a work disability rate of 25.8%; people with a high school degree (12 years of schooling) had a work disability rate of 12.3%; and people with a college degree (16 years or more of schooling) had a work disability rate of 4.8%. Some people may drop out part way through a course. The qualifications of an individual do not always match the skills employers need. Some individuals with chronic back pain have been retrained for computer workstation activity but unable to sit for prolonged periods of time after undergoing the retraining. Increased disability can result from remaining unemployed despite going through a rehabilitation process, with concomitant disappointment and loss of self esteem.

Chapter Five

Variables Contributing to the Cost of Injuries

Out of the crooked timber of humanity no straight thing can ever be made.

—Immanuel Kant, 1784

BACKGROUND

As designed, the Workers' Compensation system provides a model of excellent care for acute traumatic work-related injury. As originally conceived, injury was envisioned to be physical in nature, such as a laceration, sprain, or fracture. Following the establishment of this system, the laws were composed in order to accommodate this definition and, as such, they perform quite well under these types of circumstance. However, through time, other types of injury were added, to include such injuries as that of repetitive trauma, overuse syndrome, and non-specific pain syndromes. A set of standardized guidelines for either the management or treatment of these relatively nebulous disorders does not exist, thus enabling any given worker that presents with a complaint or feels ill in the workplace to claim an "injury," and thus seek out treatment. Treatment of these types of disorders can frequently involve a prolonged period for what can only be considered a poorly diagnosed problem, frequently resulting in iatrogenic disease and accompanying disability.

Nationally, all medical treatment in the year 2000 accounted for approximately $1.2 trillion (40), or 13 percent of the Gross Domestic Product (GDP) ($9.9 trillion), with medical costs for Workers' Compensation in California representing 45 percent of total loss payments during the same year.

Nationwide, despite the rate of injury having shown a steady decline over the past decade, a continued pattern of increases in the total amount paid per indemnity claim has been observed. In California, the Workers' Compensation Insurance Rating Bureau (48) has noted an increase in the ultimate total loss per indemnity claim from that of $17,466 in 1990 to $45,000 in 2001, an increase of 257 percent over the 10-year period, further estimating that medical costs will rise to a total of $8.2 billion in 2003.

A study conducted by the California Commission on Health and Safety (November 2002) demonstrated when medical treatment is under the control of the worker, a 7.9 percent higher cost is incurred than that in which a worker presenting with the identical condition receives treatment through an employer-selected physician or medical care provider.

Discussions with claims adjusters and insurers indicate that treatment administered through employer-selected physicians is rarely held in dispute through formal legalized processes. Conversely, the employee-selected physicians are more likely to find themselves embroiled in some type of conflict with the insurers in regard to the definition of necessary and appropriate treatment regimens and what disorders or disabilities they represent. The major proportion of litigation involving medical treatment includes those employees who assumed responsibility for selection of their primary care physicians and have retained legal representation.

The increase in medical costs is generated through three primary mechanisms: an increase in the price of a specific service; a change in present services from a category of less expensive to more expensive, often including a newly-added offering; and, an increase in utilization. Utilization refers to the use of medical services that are available

The Workers' Compensation system is primarily reliant upon the application of utilization review and dispute resolution to contain costs and provide fee schedule guidelines. In the California Workers' Compensation system, claims averaging less than 1 percent proceed to a formal hearing as the means for determining an issue of medical treatment (93). While a large number of claims involve no treatment after 30 days, the preponderance of incurred medical costs involves treatment delivered following the initial 30 days of injury (41, 42). Treatment for lower-back injuries is terminated after 30 days in 90 percent of the cases, accounting for approximately 20 to 30 percent of all injuries. That fact aside, the majority of costs derive from those claims that last beyond a 30-day period.

Thirty percent of medical costs for lower-back injuries are attributed to physical therapy treatment (39). Furthermore, 75 percent of lower-back injures require less than 4 visits, yet 90 percent of costs associated with physical therapy treatment are incurred on those claims requiring more than 4 visits.

Continual medical research is conducted in the development of new drug therapies and technologies for treatment of conditions and disorders, with a portion of these treatments frequently involving more expensive services. Physicians, therefore, might elect to utilize the least cost-effective treatment due to its ability to generate higher income revenues (94). Furthermore, unscrupulous health care providers provide excessive treatment for secondary gain such as excessive prescribing of medication, unnecessary office visits, and failing to discharge the patient in a timely manner.

Roughly 70 percent of the population will, on average, experience at the minimum one somatic symptom in any given one-week period. For the large majority of these cases, causation is indeterminate in nature. In approximately 30 percent of the cases in which patients with accompanying somatic symptoms attend a clinic, no organic cause is either discovered or determined. A study conducted by Blazer and Houpt (100) noted that the elderly subjects residing in the community perceived themselves to be of poor health, despite their not displaying any significant physical impairment. This can probably be explained on the basis of individuals experiencing the "normal" pains of daily living and are insignificant to the physical well being of the individual. Undoubtedly, there are forces present in our daily lives, like television advertising of the latest entity for which the advertised medication is needed; or the Cancer Society warning us to pay attention to anything out of the ordinary. By the way, all the cancer warning signs are late signs of advanced disease leaving little chance for cure. It has been estimated that about 20% of the population are suggestible, i.e. prone for hypochondriasis.

EMOTIONAL DISORDERS

Evidence exists that general medicine providers are well-aware of and acknowledge the small percentage of patients plagued with psychiatric disorders (50, 19, 20). However, some percentage of practicing physicians regard their only objective to include the prevention, detection, and treatment of *physical* disease—their only role in medicine is that of healer of physically-based disorders, disease, and/or symptomatology. These medical providers are of the perspective that the management of what is often termed hypochondriacal patients is both a difficult and vastly unrewarding activity.

The Whitley Index is a scale for determining levels of hypochondria. Those patients whose scores are in the higher-level ranges of this index migrate from one physician to another at a higher rate of frequency than do other patients. The individual medical histories of such patients deemed to be hypochondriacal reveal a multiplicity of diagnoses by a variety of physicians over the course of a patient's complaints. In some instances, these patients are observed to have been administered treatment for a determined physical illness until such time as subsequent medical examinations reveal their symptomatology to be innocuous in nature, thus requiring no medical treatment.

The various means at the disposal of a physician to deal with patients demonstrating *abnormal illness behaviors* (72) often involve likewise *abnormal treatment behaviors*, which can often include an inadvertent reinforcement of patient conduct, and resulting in what is termed *iatrogenic invalidism*. Iatrogenic is defined as any adverse condition in a patient occurring as a result of treatment by a health practitioner (176). The administration of unnecessary medical treatments and protocols can often lead to drug-induced complications and not uncommonly side-effects, perhaps life-threatening or reaching perilous levels in some cases which, in turn, lead to an entirely new set of symptomatological complaints. An intricate and often difficult to resolve scenario at best, and evolving into a labyrinthine dilemma comprised of costly legal and medical issues at worst.

The hypochondriacal patient will often present with several persistent somatic symptoms. Following a series of examinations and investigative studies, a minor abnormality is often discovered, for which treatment is attempted by the physician, based upon the assumption that the abnormality might play a contributory role in this host of symptoms. The physically healthy individual with accompanying psychological problems, fraught with worry and concern surrounding his/her somatic symptoms, is now in possession of yet another worry: the belief that they are no longer a healthy individual, with the risk of this occurring increasing geometrically as the patient vacillates back and forth between one provider and another, forever seeking resolution to their confusing array of symptoms.

These patients eventually encounter a physician who misinterprets these symptoms and findings to be evidentiary of and based on an underlying disease. The diagnosis heard by a majority of these patients is often more grave in tone than that which the physician in actuality conveys, with treatment confirming this flawed belief that there does, indeed, exist a physical disorder.

The larger majority of patients have difficulty in understanding the relationship that exists between the emotional base and somatic symptoms as applicable to their own situation. These relationships, which are often remote and difficult to determine by trained professionals, are incomprehensible by magnitudes far greater in level to the layperson, who is often anxiety-ridden and bewildered at their predicament.

Patients who fall into this category might be examined in a clinic catering to the practice of industrial medicine, and the vigilant clinician would do well to recognize the characteristic traits of patients in this group, preempting further problems with early detection appropriate management techniques. In consideration of the ability of these types of problems to contribute greatly to the high rate of medical costs and expenditures, it is only pragmatic to not simply be alert to these patients, but to possess the necessary skills for which to cost-effectively formulate and manage the treatment of these patients.

SIMULATION DISORDERS

Other disorders leading at times to unnecessary medical expenditures can include:

• Malingering
• Factitious Disorders
• Compensation Neurosis

These categories will be further discussed in Chapters 8 and 9. They are disorders that have in common the false or grossly exaggerated presentation of symptoms, or false attribution of physical or mental disorders. The clinician must distinguish not only between health and illness but also between health imitating illness and illness imitating health. Diagnosis of simulation disorders is by exclusion of physical disease most of the time and consumes costly testing and repeated evaluations.

DIAGNOSTIC STUDIES

Diagnostic studies are generally considered to be high-cost generators. Nowadays, it appears that an increasing number of patients are demanding imaging studies as follow-up to injury in order to determine whether there might exist an occult medical problem. This type of quite expensive technology has only become widely available in recent years, and a majority of patients view these medically advanced technologies as means by which to be deemed cleared medically following an injury. Baseline X-rays are frequently performed following injuries as insurance in today's prevailing medical-legal environment. Those employees presenting with hand or wrist pain often demand electrodiagnostic studies to determine if perhaps the cause of their discomfort is due to carpal tunnel syndrome, a disorder that is often associated with repetitive motion trauma as an outcome of work-related activity. The Bureau of Labor Statistics reported about 28,000 cases of carpal tunnel syndrome in 1999. So many people have surgery for this condition that it is the leading cause of lost workdays. Half of all people who suffer from this condition miss 30 or more days of work per year, and the average cost is more than $13,000 per case (177).

As distinguished from traditional medical health insurance, the Workers' Compensation system requires neither a deductible nor a co-payment on the part of the injured worker. Rather, it is highly improbable that the worker will reject, due to exorbitant costs, any testing procedures or treatment modalities recommended, as might be the case with a non-work-related injury. What might be deemed unnecessary, or excessively cost-prohibitive medical treatment, is now considered to be readily acceptable in the Workers' Compensation program.

REHABILITATION

Another source of high cost generation involves the process of physical rehabilitation from the injury. Physical medicine services, such as manipulations and adjustments, supervised exercise, hot and cold packs, electro stimulation and massage accounts for approximately 20 to 30 percent of total medical costs in several regions throughout the United States (183). This encompasses physical therapy and chiropractic care. Vocational rehabilitation, which involves retraining for another job when an individual is unable to return to their present job, is an integral part of many workers' compensation programs. In a 1988 study, vocational rehabilitation in Florida was involved in 18% of lost-time cases, in California the comparable number was 9%. In New York, where rehabilitation was voluntary, only 2% of cases received these services. In the 1988 study, 60% of participants completed the rehabilitation program in Florida with a return to work rate of 77% (178). Costs in the period studied were $53 million representing 8 cents of every benefit dollar. In California, costs were 30% higher due to emphasis on more expensive schooling and training programs, but the return to work rate was only 69%. Recent data from the Minnesota Department of Labor and Industry revealed that in 2001, 21 per cent of claims used this service with a return to work average of 73 per cent, at a cost of 37.1 $million for 6,700 workers (181).

Among people with no disability, 82.1% are employed. People who have any functional limitations, 32.2% are employed (184). According to the Survey of Income and Program Participation (SIPP), 32.1 million working age people (15-64) have a disability, which is almost 20 per cent of the work group (184). However, the likelihood of having a job with a non-severe disability is 76.9%, but with a severe disability it is 26.1%.

LITIGATION

Legal fees associated with Workers' Compensation claims increases costs by approximately 12 to 15 percent, and are involved in 5 to 10 percent of all such claims, and in one-third of those claims in which the worker has been absent from work (16). Attorney involvement is not necessarily indication of a formal litigation process. However, those times do occur in which the worker will seek an attorney to assist in the negotiation process that involves, at times, a confusing and complex system structure.

The steep rise in litigation rates (85) has been well-documented over the course of the past decade. In California, with litigation costs averaging $2.2 billion in 1992, reform legislation was introduced and enacted as a means for controlling this massive increase in expenditures.

Litigation involves the legal filing of a claim by at least one party to an ongoing dispute. To some degree, litigation has become a customary feature in the Workers' Compensation system since its inception. In order to qualify for Workers' Compensation, it is mandatory that an injury be shown to be work-related in nature. This, then, opens the door to potential dispute. Benefit payments are directly linked to physical impairment, the degree of which might be disputed as well.

The underlying tenets of the Workers' Compensation laws (33) are mainly concerned with income maintenance and equitability. A compensation system dependent upon the judicial court system would be incapable of accomplishing this due to the inevitable delays associated with the process, as witnessed during the period prior to the establishment of the Workers' Compensation system. During that era, injured workers were subjected to prolonged periods of severe income interruption. Within the framework of the tort system, it was necessary that employer negligence be proven in order to establish employer liability, a difficult activity at best to prove in a court of law. Jury-awarded compensation varied widely, often involving protracted delays between the time of injury and determination of award.

It is not, therefore, unreasonable to question whether the increase in litigation has also equally compromised the effectiveness of the program. The impact of litigation imposes an element of friction into the equation, draining resources and, ultimately, resulting in a loss in productivity of goods and services.

Studies reveal that the body part experiencing injury as well as the type of injury can affect the probability of future litigation. Injuries deemed difficult to objectively evaluate, such as those incurring back-related impairment, or multiple-level injuries, can serve to increase the probability of litigation as well. The age of the worker as well as the industry in which he or she is employed both serve to affect the probability of litigation. Employment in the manufacturing and construction sectors increase the probability of litigious activity, while those employed within the services industries will work toward decreasing litigious probability. The greater the difficulty or ambiguity of estimating the level of impairment, the more likelihood there is of the probability of litigation.

Legal disputes can be divided into four phases, as follows:

Phase 1: An event occurring in which one party injures another (occurrence of a lost-time injury.)

Phase 2: The injured party determines whether to assert a legal claim.

Phase 3: The pretrial discovery period, in which expert medical opinion is solicited to determine the extent of injury and impairment to employee.

Phase 4: A court-imposed solution to the dispute is rendered should parties be unable to reach mutual agreement.

LOST PRODUCTIVITY

In a survey, conducted by Liberty Mutual Insurance Company in 2001 (36), "Executive Survey of Workplace Safety," the information gathered suggests that the disabling injuries suffered by workers incurred direct costs of $40 billion during 1999, along with an additional $80 to $200 billion in other injury-related costs. The estimate of the other costs was gleaned from findings that 56 percent of executives are in agreement that indirect costs ranged anywhere from $2 to $5 for every dollar expended in direct costs, primarily resulting from lost productivity based on the lost-revenue calculation.

TERTIARY GAIN

Those third parties benefiting from an individual worker's injury might realize tertiary gain. An entire industry has developed comprised of tertiary beneficiaries, to include medical professionals, allied health workers, insurance case managers, rehabilitation counselors, and lawyers representing both sides of the dispute.

The response of many patients to tertiary gain is through means of augmentation and exaggeration of symptomatology. Should the patient receive no response to the symptoms from the treatment physician, the solution is remedied by shifting providers. Some physicians assign blame for resulting poor patient outcomes to the lawyers, as though the lawyer demanded the patient not respond to treatment. They point to even worse surgical results stemming from Workers' Compensation litigants. While Workers' Compensation patients have been known to report significant levels of depression and anxiety, the litigating patients appear to experience less distress than non-litigants (Tait, Chibnall, & Richardson, 1990). One might here conjecture that litigation can serve as a coping mechanism of sorts for distressed patients, in response to the adversarial nature of the Workers' Compensation system.

CHRONIC PAIN

When failing to appropriately care for chronic pain patients, healthcare providers inadvertently add to the difficulties, thus increasing the patient's problems, often including a sense of confusion, frustration, and hopelessness. Some commonly observed problems are cited by Beck and Lusting (1990), as follows:

• Healthcare provides are hard-put to believe patients who present with pain symptoms in the absence of pathology.
• Chronic pain is often treated using the acute pain model.
• A tendency exists to both underestimate and overestimate the gravity of iatrogenic drug addiction.
• Placebos are often used incorrectly.
• Patients are not often referred to psychological or counseling services until other strategies have been exhausted or failed to ameliorate the problem.

FITNESS FOR DUTY

Pre-placement or pre-screening evaluations should be performed as a means for weeding out those individuals who are deemed as experiencing potential difficulties in performing the job-related duties. This device is used primarily to protect both the employer and employee, militating against the potential filing of claims by employees, and serving as a defense system to protect the worker from work-related injuries.The examination serves the following primary purposes (133):

1. To determine the individual's ability to perform a specific job.
2. To perform an assessment of the individual's general health.
3. To establish a baseline or benchmark for purposes of surveillance and medical/legal purposes.

In my professional capacity, I have been witness to many individuals with pre-existing medical disorders or some form of physical limitation or debilitation, applying for a position that will prove potentially harmful to them. Thus, it seems only prudent that, through the use of the occupational medicine provider, the employer make a determination as to the suitability and fitness for duty of the prospective employee. As the physician, however, the hiring decision does not rest within your jurisdiction, but that of the employer's. However, the physician's role includes the responsibility to offer recommendations on employee placement, with the employer assuming the role of final arbiter as to whether the recommendations can be reasonably accommodated. The legal basis for this stems from both the Rehabilitation Act of 1973, applicable to Federal agencies and their contractors, and the Americans with Disabilities Act (ADA), applicable to civilians. Acting as the agent for the employer, the physician can and will be held responsible and accountable for any act of wrongdoing or appearance of such.

In recording a patient's medical history, along with the more general medical questions, one might find the following questions to be invaluable in helping to detect either a prior injury or disability determination:

1. Have you had any previous injuries that are unresolved, or that have caused any impairments or restrictions?
2. Do you have any medical illnesses, or diagnoses, that are unresolved? And, if so, do these cause any physical or mental restrictions or impairments?
3. Have you had any surgeries? If so, are there any permanent liabilities remaining?
4. Have you ever experienced any psychiatric problems or diagnosis?
5. Have you currently or in the recent past been prescribed medications or treatment strategies for any problem?
6. Do you perceive any limitations in your ability to perform work-related activities?

I verify that all the above information is correct and understand that the provision of false, misleading, or incomplete information might be grounds for disciplinary action up to and including termination. (This attestation can act as a deterrent the applicant providing false information or omissions in its provision for a penalty to be levied should an act of commission be observed.)

These questions might appear to be somewhat redundant in nature; however, it is an attempt to detect information that the worker might not otherwise wish to disclose. As example, let us suppose that a worker had in fact experienced a prior injury in which a permanent lifting restriction of a maximum of 50 lbs. was determined. The position he is presently applying for carries with the requirement of occasional lifting of up to 75 lbs., yet no pre-placement evaluation or pre-screening measures are requested by the employer. The worker is thus hired and, in the performance of the newly-acquired work-related activities, he or she is injured. The question then becomes, how would this worker be capable of returning to a position for which he or she was not initially qualified? A permanent partial disability rating as well as costs associated with vocational rehabilitation would no doubt ensue, further causing high rates of unnecessary costs and preventable injuries.

In sum, determinations regarding job capacity must rest within the purview of a medically-rendered decision. Any attempt to eliminate this judgment factor has the potential to result in unnecessary rejections or poor placement decisions.

THE EMPLOYER'S REPRESENTATIVE

In order to defend against the act of malingering, the employer engages the active involvement of an employer representative (65). Waiting for the insurance company to act might well result in loss of control of the case, thus direct transport of the employee to the physician should be carried out by the employer's representative. If an objection is raised or voiced by the employee or physician, the representative is in the position of being able to offer explanation that this requirement has been established as a means to ensure Workers' Compensation compliance, in addition to ensuring sufficient enough manpower for the employer, and to interface directly with the insurance carrier in determining that all benefits and medical costs are being covered.

The representative should avert any excuses to not visiting a doctor offered by the employee. If the employee has retained attorney representation, the employer's representative can then request a second opinion. If the employee has already secured a physician, the representative can then accompany him or her to the next appointment and further request any information pertaining to physician diagnosis, return-to-work status issues, and reasonable treatment recommendations.

In any event, a personalized follow-up meeting should be conducted with the employee on a once-a-week basis, the purpose of which is to ensure the employee is cognizant of his movements being monitored closely. Follow-up contact with the claims adjuster is recommended to provide information concerning issues concerning return-to-work time frames, hopefully at a date as early as is possible.

Anecdotal evidence also suggests the ability of such techniques to reduce the rate of malingering claims by approximately 70 percent. The more expeditiously a worker is returned to normal work-related activity, the lower the compensation insurance premiums. Assuming a proactive interest and role in the claims process by the employer will demonstrate to employees that, not only have monitoring procedures to detect fraudulent behavior been set in place, but that an important ally exists who cares sufficiently enough to focus personal attention to a bona fide work-related injury.

THE SUPERVISOR

There sometimes exists an abundance of both conflicting and characteristic dysfunction between the relationship between supervisors and workers, the results of which can often lead to a highly toxic work environment leading to more destructive outcomes. Conflict between worker and supervisor can best be described as a condition existing between two people, in which at least one party experiences anger, resentment, and hostility toward the other, is critical of the other party's actions, leading to a disruption of effective and productive work-related activity and workplace morale (179). In short, the leading cause of conflict in the workplace environment is attributed to interpersonal relationships and the stress-related conduct as exhibited in the work environment. These stressors can in turn lead all too frequently to higher rates of accident, injury, or illness, resulting in further lost time and sizable decrease in productivity.

Thus, it would appear imperative that employers learn the methods for identifying dysfunctional workplace interrelationships, their underlying causes and origins, and the means and strategies by which to prevent their occurrence. Supervisors are in need of training in areas of conflict resolution, consisting of a specific set of readily-learned methods that are carefully designed to conjoin the two disputing parties in a reasonable process allowing for resolution and mutual satisfaction.

By allowing for the training of workplace managers in the use of these methodologies, employers can perform interdiction in costly workplace disputes, often seen to result in high rates of absenteeism, reduced productivity levels, and the probability and potential for future exorbitant litigation. Conflict resolution in the workplace has been proven to significantly reduce accident rates, loss of workday time, and counterproductive behaviors causing disruption in harmonious and productivity-oriented workplaces.

INSURANCE

The employer's premium rate for Workers' Compensation Insurance is reflective of the relative hazards workers are exposed to along with the claim record history of the employer. Roughly one-quarter of the States make allowances for what is termed a "schedule rating," which is a discount or rate credit applied to those employers who have been deemed to have established superior workplace safety programs. In addition, the large majority of States currently provide the option of medical deductibles for these employers as a cost-saving measure. Deductibles, which the employer is required to pay, serve as encouragement for the employer to establish greater levels of safety awareness in the workplace environment,

PERMANENT DISABILITY

In California, cumulative trauma and permanent disability injuries, are two types of injury viewed to be particularly troublesome. Both injuries can become mired in protracted delays and postponements through the litigation process. Permanent disability claims occur at twice the national average in California's employee population. While, the settlements received by these employees is below most standard compensatory awards—only 68 percent of the national average, an astonishing fact considering its occurrence in a state in which the cost of living is higher than that of the national average, according to the National Council on Compensation Insurance.

Despite having been no official change made to the ratings guidelines, California has experienced a steady increase in average ratings from the Disability Evaluation Unit in recent years. Ranging from the period 1992 through 1996, an overall 14 percent increase occurred in the impairment rating for back injuries, a 16 percent increase for upper-extremity ratings, and a 3 percent differential noted between ratings for the same condition in Northern California than that of Southern California (115). The litigation process, along with increased expenditures, are natural consequences of low levels of reliability, and the ancillary costs flowing from that.

The contentious nature of permanent disability issues rests in the difficulty arising from rendering determinations as to what percentage of impairment has been sustained by an injured worker. Often, two different workers who present with disabilities identical in nature will be assigned different disability percentages. The Rand Institute for Civil Justice conducted a study in which it was found that the ratings for permanent disability below 25% (which totals 90 percent of claims) provide low validity rates in that no consistent relationship can be established between the ratings and wage loss factors.

California's Permanent Disability Rating Schedule specifies standard percentage rates for permanent impairments and limitations, and further provides for the modification of these standardized ratings based upon age factors and occupation. The standard rating is age-adjusted by decreasing the rating for younger workers, while attaching an increased rating for the older workers, based on the theory that those in the younger-worker range more adequately adjust and adapt to permanent disability or handicap than do the older workers. The standard rating is adjusted to accommodate specific occupation by increasing the ratings if the limitations are viewed as posing more of an impediment to job performance in that particular labor industry.

On average, 60 percent of permanently injured workers in California receive disability ratings below 15 percent, according to the California Applicants' Attorneys Association. In 2002, the upper limit allowed for workers to receive is $140.00 per week for a total of 49.25 weeks, totaling $6,895 over the course ranging throughout almost one year. For example, in 2002, the rating for a California worker is deemed to be 100 percent permanent disability, he or she will receive two-thirds salary for the remainder of his or her lifetime, not to exceed more than $490 per week, or $25,480 per year (97).

In the case of a worker who has been rated at less than 100 percent disability, the payment amount is calculated as follows: two-thirds of the average weekly wage, with a maximum payment of $140 per week if rated to be below 15 percent disabled, $160 if rated to be below 24.75 percent disabled, $170 per week if rated to be below 69.75% disabled, and $230 per week if rated to be 70 percent or more disabled.

Those workers deemed to be 1 percent disabled would receive a total of three weekly payments. And, those workers determined to be 99.75 percent disabled would receive payments for a total of 694.25 weeks, or approximately 13 years.

In a majority of States in which the statues provide benefits totaling two-thirds of a worker's salary, many employees receive benefit amounts that total an amount greater than two-thirds of their lost income, owing to the tax-free stipulation of Workers' Compensation benefits. Tax-free benefits are greater in value for those workers who fall within higher tax brackets. In general, most workers in a given state receive between 80 and 100 percent of their after-tax income (118) in temporary disability benefits. Added savings of avoiding "going to work expenses" contribute to this calculation, as well as the employer continuing to pay for fringe benefits.

Over time, cumulative trauma injuries progress, such as those including back-related disorders and repetitive motion injury. Permanent injuries result in either permanent loss of earnings or in earning capacity, with both types raising difficult questions that require resolution for employers and insurers alike. The frequency with which these types of injury have developed in recent years, both nationwide and in California, is perhaps owing to the new categories of employment developing in a more technologically advanced society, an elevated awareness of health and safety issues, more accurate diagnostic techniques and testing procedures, and overall improvement in methods of reporting.

One fast-developing category of dispute is that of arm and wrist injuries, most likely as a reflection of the high usage of computer keyboarding and lengthier periods of time spent in the performance of office-related activities.

The most commonly-disputed injury from the period of 1991 to 1996 on the Northern Coast of California was that of back injuries, more than 90 percent of the time proceeding to litigation (32). Those claims comprised one-third of all disputed claims due to the inherent distrust insurers displayed as to the validity of the types of claims.

On a more philosophical level, 75 percent of the 800 employers surveyed by the Workers' Compensation Institute in 1990 were of the belief that workers should not receive compensation for permanent disabilities if they return to work. In their perspective, these workers are engaging in the identical work-related activities as performed prior to their injuries. They further think that workers should not be paid permanent disability benefits if the insurer has allocated payments for vocational rehabilitation plans in order to be retained for another category of work. Simply stated, those surveyed were found to disagree with the established laws in terms of the way in which disability benefits are awarded.

The basis for which disability benefits are awarded is that of loss of function, resulting in a permanent form of physical or mental limitation or restriction, irrespective of the worker's present occupation. This determination of loss or impairment is reached by calculating a comparison of the performance ability of the worker across the boundaries of the general workforce population (90). It is a theoretical construct, which may or may not possess valid relationship to the reality of a given situation.

Impairment is defined to be the loss, loss of use, or derangement of any body part, organ system, or organ function (119). Although an impairment rating can be derived from one set of observations, it conveys no information about a given individual's capacity to meet or exceed personal, social, or occupational demands as defined by a given disability (120).

DISABILITY AWARDS

The following lists examples of disability rating percentages for a variety of injuries, along with the maximum lump-sum payments distributed in California during 2002:

Type of Injury	Rating Percentage	Payment
• Loss of sense of smell	5%	$2,100
• Loss of index finger	8%	3,360
• Loss of a great toe	10%	4,235
• Complete loss of hearing in one ear	15%	8,040
• Immobility of wrist	20%	11,280
• Loss of sight in one eye	30%	21,420
• Moderately impaired back	50%	45,263
• Loss of 5 fingers	55%	52,063
• Complete loss of hearing bilateral	60%	58,863
• Loss of one leg	65%	65,663
• Loss of hand	70%	98,095

The following lists the variations in lump-sum payments amongst several states for the loss of one eye, in 1996:

STATE	AMOUNT
Maryland	$138,195
Illinois	124,987
Iowa	108,920
Connecticut	92,473
Hawaii	80,160
Delaware	74,446
Ohio	65,125
New Hampshire	63,087
South Carolina	63,087
North Carolina	61,440
West Virginia	58,689
South Dakota	56,250
Nebraska	53,375
Wisconsin	47,850
New Jersey	47,268
Virginia	46,600
Georgia	45,000
New Jersey	47,268
Utah	42,120

continued

STATE	AMOUNT
Oregon	42,000
Tennessee	38,279
Missouri	37,621
Arizona	34,650
Idaho	32,175
Washington	30,903
Arkansas	37,405
Alabama	27,280
Mississippi	27,067
Massachusetts	22,841
California	21,420
Colorado	20,850
Rhode Island	14,400
North Dakota	2,580

Two basic methods are used by jurisdictions for determination of what is termed to be permanent partial disability (PPD) benefits. The first method uses a schedule, as indicated above, in which the benefits are listed for the loss of use of a specific body part. The second method on the other hand is based on injuries not scheduled, i.e., those injuries to the head, trunk, back, and internal organs.

For this second category of injury, most jurisdictions use one or more of the following four approaches to determine the accrued benefits:

1. Impairment—the actual physical and psychological loss produced by the injury or illness.
2. Loss of wage-earning capacity—based on an estimate of the worker's future loss of wages owing to the injury impairment.
3. Actual wage loss—the difference calculated between the earnings capacity of the worker based on pre-injury and post-injury status.
4. A bifurcated approach—benefits based upon the degree of impairment or the extent of lost wage-earning capacity, contingent upon employment status of the worker.

The interaction of other elements linked to permanent partial disability benefits, such as those involving choice of healthcare provider, extent of attorney involvement, and amount of other benefits, can work toward creating various economic incentives and/or disincentives that influence a worker's ability to transition from temporary status to that of either permanent total disability or permanent partial disability status (117). Better stated, many other factors external to the physical impairment contribute to the determination as to whether or not an injured worker returns to work.

In an NCCI survey (134), it was stated that 60 percent of all benefit costs result from permanent partial disability.

SUMMARY

Dramatic cost increases can serve to detract from the focus of policymakers and business leaders alike in tailoring high-quality and easily accessible health care to employees experiencing work-related injury. Two primary elements serve to drive up the costs of Workers' Compensation insurance (162), the first that of the administrative burden, at times referred to as the "friction" inherent in the respective State Workers' Compensation systems. Friction might best be viewed as the accumulation of rules, procedures, disputes, delays, discretionary charges, and patterns of practice that bring to bear undue pressures on the claims resolution process. The second element that fuels higher costs includes that of outcomes, in specific the success rate within a given state to prevent injuries. When these injuries do occur, the higher their rate of success in returning the injured worker to both healthful and productive normalized work-related activities will work as means to avoid prolonged absences in the workplace and costly medical treatments.

A list of strategies for implementing cost containment within the context of Workers' Compensation Medical care are listed below:

- Discounted fee schedules.
- Utilization management of Workers' Compensation medical services.
- Restricted networks of designated physicians.
- Case management.
- Mandatory treatment guidelines.
- Hospital payment regulations.

Chapter Six

Quality of Care Issues

People of quality know everything without ever having been taught anything.

—Moliere, 1660

BACKGROUND

Obtaining medical care under the Workers' Compensation system can often be a complex and somewhat daunting process encompassing issues of quality of care for the injured worker. The intricate nature of these issues includes the appropriateness and timely response of care administered, accessibility to care, level and degree of worker satisfaction of medical care, the impact of medical care and follow-up rehabilitative procedures on return to work, and recovery of worker to former job functionality.

As but one of its primary goals, the Workers' Compensation system serves to ensure the relative ease and immediacy of access to urgent medical services for on-the-job-related injuries. Notwithstanding such predominant intent, however, in endeavoring to obtain appropriate medical services in an expeditious manner one often encounters a sizably complicated maze, most especially when one considers that the worker, employer, medical provider, and insurer must work in cohesion within the framework of coordinated activities involving innumerable medical judgments and administrative levels. For example, in order to qualify for compensatory benefits, a worker's presenting illness or injury must first be established as job-related along with the mandated filing of claims reports. The worker is deemed responsible for the se-

74

lection of medical provider, often among several eligible and available, to seek treatment as provided by the guidelines of his or her employer's insurance policy. Medical care providers are required to know which services are allowable under Workers' Compensation insurance, as well as what administrative reporting requirements must be adhered to. Both the insurer and claims administrators are required as well to conform to those statutes and regulations directly relevant to the given case at-hand, so that one set of guidelines might not of necessity be applicable in all injury-related cases.

Any denial of benefits by an insurer deriving from a Workers' Compensation claim is considered to be a potential barrier to accessibility of medical care, the consequences of which can be of such magnitude as to imperil the worker's ability to receive appropriate treatment should he or she not be in possession of alternative forms of health coverage.In some cases, injured workers might exhibit reluctance to report work-related injuries, several reasons of which are listed below:

1. Fear of employer reprisals.
2. Intimated by fear of job loss.
3. Language and cultural barriers, generally witnessed amongst those workers for whom English is a second language.
4. Lack of information and knowledge regarding compensation benefits.
5. Disruption to employer safety record, in which rewards are allocated for installed safety incentive programs.

PROGRAM VARIATIONS

A variety of studies have demonstrated wide differentials to exist amongst States in the usage of health services for specific conditions as treated under their respective Workers' Compensation programs (127). Following suit, where variation in care exists, one often discovers likewise wide variation in quality of that care as well. Dr. James Tacci et al., in a study of clinical practices of the management of low back workers' compensation claims in 1999, identified the frequently evidenced overuse of diagnostic imaging studies, variations in the use of prescription drugs, and high usage of therapeutic modalities that have no documented proven effectiveness (128). In yet another study, it was found that, although surgery for back-related injuries often demonstrates improvement over the long-term, those workers receiving Workers' Compensation benefits were less likely to undergo these surgical procedures than those not in receipt of Workers' Compensation benefits (129).

One of the preeminent functions assumed by Workers' Compensation benefits is that of minimizing the economic loss to both the injured employee and the employer, while endeavoring to maximize both the functional and vocational recovery levels of the worker. Of particular concern to individual States has been the historical rise in Workers' Compensation program costs, which have sizably exceeded that of group health medical costs for reasons including but not limited to cost-shifting, case-shifting, and the high volume and intensity of services and benefits provided throughout the course of the disability. As a result, a major issue surrounding Workers' Compensation programs is that involving cost control while simultaneously working diligently to improve accessibility to and quality of medical care. As contrasted to group health medical care services, Workers ' Compensation programs have limited ability to undertake the establishment of standardization of protocols nor formulated guidelines to optimize quality of care and promote the efficiency of the system (131, 132).

STANDARDS

Within the general health care setting, several approaches have been developed for the measurement and improvement of quality of care, including:

• Continuous quality improvement programs.
• Research conducted into the outcomes of care.
• Development of quality indicators
• Performance benchmarks
• Consumer-oriented satisfaction and functional measures.
• Introduction of treatment guidelines.

Overall, Workers' Compensation programs have achieved little if any success via the introduction of utilization control mechanisms, while successful results are evidenced in the group health benefit environment with programs such as HMOs and Preferred Provider Networks optimally utilizing such measures as risk-sharing. In contrast, the Workers' Compensation system is more reliant upon mechanisms, such as that of fee schedules, in which the program maintains unit price control of services, and that of utilization review, as means by which to control the units and types of service delivery. States such as Florida and New Hampshire, in which managed care programs have been established, have achieved variable degrees of cost reduction, albeit along with a majority of employees generally perceived to be less satisfied with the quality of medical care under arrangements of this type. One preeminent measure of the level of quality of a given health care delivery system is that of the satisfaction of the population it purports to serve, without which the program must be viewed overall as either sadly deficient or an outright failure. The Workers' Compensation system, if viewed from this vantage point, falls into this category and demands improvements on a wide-ranging scale.

Traditionally, consumers do not generally display interest in high-level technical measurements, instead focusing their attention and individual concerns on matters that revolve around the extent of eligible benefits, provider selection and choice, accessibility to care, the quality of available services, and associated costs (130). Injured workers, on the other hand, distinctively different in their behavioral norms than other health consumers, are often either ill-informed or sadly wholly uninformed regarding the overall processes that constitute the Workers' Compensation system. Injured workers often harbor anger, primarily leveled at their employers, in large measure owing to safety hazards encountered in the workplace. These employees often display lowered levels of expectations relating to health care and worker-related benefits, an indicative instrument of their predisposed notions of a system that decidedly does not have their best interests as its focus. There is a marked behavioral and attitudinal tenor and tone to the injured worker that bespeaks a level of resignation—an inherent distrust in a system that will favor its own needs above that of the injured employee.

PAST ANALYSIS

In 2000, the California Division of Workers' Compensation (DWC) presided over focus group discussions on health care quality for the injured worker population of the California Workers' Compensation system, with sessions conducted on an individual basis respectively with the following groups: injured workers, employers, physicians, nurse case managers, claims adjusters, applicants' attorneys, DWC judges, and information/assistant officers. Agreement was reached by the majority of participants that *functional outcomes* and *return-to-work plans* are areas and issues most in need of both attention and improvement as related to quality of health care for Workers' Compensation participants. The following list delineates suggested improvements to the quality of care for those who comprise the work-related injured population:

1. To provide more *information* for injured workers, employers, and providers regarding all elements of medical care within the Workers' Compensation system.

2. To improve *accountability* by instituting performance measures for participating health care providers.
3. To require *certification* for those physicians who provide treatment within
   the Workers' Compensation system.
4. To improve *training* for claims adjusters, and work toward improving their
   workload levels.
5. To change *financial* incentives by encouraging all parties to make it prior-
   ity to attain high-quality care and positive outcomes for workers.
6. To encourage a return to work through employer *incentives* or requirements, as well as physician training.
7. To provide an Ombudsman, or intermediary, for injured workers who is
   capable of furnishing pertinent information and to serve in the capacity as
   an aide in the prevention of future litigation.

How does this relate to our present discussion and what can be inferred
from the above-suggested recommendations to the Workers' Compensation
system? Objectively viewed, for all purposes, this indicates that the system is
operational and functioning, albeit ineffectively, and in dire need of repair and
refurbishing, when one considers the increasing costs and diminishing levels
of returns on investment. These increased costs, passed through to the employer in the form of higher insurance premiums rates, in conjunction with
lower levels of worker productivity, are in turn passed on and ultimately
transferred to the consumer. Thus, we as a population are those held most responsible for bearing the burden of the increasing levels of inefficiency and
widespread inequities in which the system is entrenched. Certainly, by all accounts, an unacceptable scenario, and one for which the populace is not only
burdened by wide disparities in costs proportionate to inadequate levels of
medical care quality, but reduction in emotional and physical recovery rates
for the injured workers. The cause and effect ratio as related to worker
productivity produces wide-reaching negative impacts on entire industries, a
fact that cannot be disputed and one in which immediate attention need be
focused.

Presently, few incentives exist to facilitate improvements to the system.
When the far easier approach entails simply continuing with the present
agenda rather than the arduous and complicated task of instigating and instituting change, what impetus remains to alter such a traditionally embedded
non-growth-oriented system? Entire industries have sprung from, progressed,
and continued to evolve and transform, indeed fostering livelihoods completely dependent upon, by virtue of these self-same inefficiencies and inad-
equacies that comprise the Workers' Compensation system. Thus, a vehement
resistance exists to perform much-needed alterations to that system. Further,

there exists a general sentiment of distrust amidst the different factions, forming a concrete barrier to quality improvement. If perceived to be threats to the very livelihood of those for whom the system has provided such lucrative sustenance, what possible inspiration exists to engage in change?

The pervasive distrust that enfolds the Workers' Compensation system can be viewed as a byproduct of both the society and cultural norms and era inhabited by the vast majority of our population. The ideologies that formed the foundation for and derived the concept of long-term employment security is now a long-gone and forgotten ideal existent only as vague memory, along with the dedication to job and company that accompanied that ideal. The ever-transitional employment climate currently evident in society acts a deterrent to company loyalty, an ideal both abundant in and well-expected throughout previous periods in American society. Employees shift jobs and careers with ease, all the more facilitating the notion that loyalty, diligence, and focus on the growth and development of one company, within the context of perhaps a singular industry, comprise a fading ideal no longer viable in twenty-first century America. This brutal truth regarding the corporate culture of America in today's society only adds in breadth and depth to the problematic nature of implementing improvements and change to a static system, such as that of Workers' Compensation.

Both the concept and implementation of Managed Health Care appear to have greatly contributed to this wide-reaching attitude, with increasing sentiments voiced amongst patients who perceive the need to *demand* rather than expect appropriate medical care as a natural outgrowth of a system purported to have the best interests of the patient at its core. The very concept that patients are required to voice such demands indicates a troublesome and highly inadequate system. The expectations that a system will be sorely lacking in its ability to minister high-quality and appropriate medical care conveys to the populace all the earmarks of a broken system, one that has failed to achieve its originally mandated purposes.

Save for customary word-of-mouth modes of communication, no guidelines exist as assistance to the worker regarding issues such as whether the medical provider is following appropriate protocol for management of a given disorder. Little or no information is available in matters regarding expected treatment outcomes as means for guiding the consumer in discerning and determining informed medical decisions. In some cases, contracts to providers are awarded based not upon merit but degree of political connectedness, despite known abuses of both utilization and services. In occurrences such as these, when cost containment is the watchword, this type of behavior demonstrates wholesale ignorance on the part of decision-makers regarding the observable existing correlation between cost control and quality improvement factors.

In cases where payment is made for remedies that have proven efficacy, for instance, as in evidence-based medicine, funds are not unnecessarily squandered on those services and treatments without having first established a given protocol's proven benefits. The paucity of health care funding is the propellant force behind the current movement in traditional medical care. The insurance industry has made attempts at oversight of Workers' Compensation expenditures, but their hands are unfortunately tied due to uninformed adjusters as well as the system it has attempted to improve. Billing review companies are employed to scrutinize invoicing procedures, however, the magnitude of the problem and its attaching laws serve to radically handicap these efforts.

Numerous rationales can be offered as to why workers are not amenable to closing their claims. Often inhibited by fear of exacerbated future ramifications deriving from the injury, workers are paralyzed by the notion that they will be unable to reopen their case should they so desire at a later date. They are of the belief that an underlying serious illness or injury might be obscured to the eye of the medical provider, thus it will be misdiagnosed and overlooked, potentially causing future unforeseen difficulties. In some cases, workers demonstrate disappointment in the system being predicated on a no-fault basis, and strongly desire just compensation, as exists in cases adjudicated in civil court proceedings, for what they perceive to be endurance of undeserved pain and suffering. Prolonged care and follow-up treatments and therapies contribute to a level of wastefulness and often-unneeded expenditures. It has long been noted that the general attitude amongst injured workers is one of indifference to whether significant fiscal waste is inherent in their medical care costs. The widespread prevalence of entitlement that so pervades our culture serves to enhance worker sentiment that they are deserving of compensation in cases of injury due to job-related activities, thus no expenditure need be spared in the remediation of this problem. Despite the understanding that much-needed improvements are demanded by a highly inefficacious system, and the that there does not exist an unremitting bounty of funds in which to compensate injury-related workers in each and every case, the generalized perceptions of the system as being a trough from which to endlessly feed serves as powerful inducement to employee misuse and abuse.

SURVEYS

The Medical Provider is only capable of controlling those elements of the system that fall within the domain of his or her jurisdiction. In this vein, several parameters are currently used to assess the quality of care as practiced throughout clinical settings, through the establishment of benchmark procedures and devices, and include the following:

- Injured worker satisfaction survey
- Client (employer) satisfaction survey
- Insurance company satisfaction survey
- Percentage of patient referrals to medical specialists
- Percentage of First-Aid cases
- Percentage of patient referrals to Physical Therapists
- Percentage of injured workers who have not returned to work

Instances of having performed our services at an effective level of medical care do exist, thus we logically discharge the patient from the system, utilizing all expected criteria and parameters of sound medical treatment, yet the worker acclaims a recurrence of symptoms, the consequence of which is his or her transitioning to another medical provider. The patient has now moved beyond our control, venturing off to yet another path unbeknownst to us. Practitioners of Occupational Medicine rarely if ever in possession of complete confidence regarding medical outcomes, laden as our profession is with limitations set forth by insurance companies in the type and level of information that can be communicated to the public, and often almost entirely attributable to medical confidentiality laws. These strictures can introduce extremely detrimental elements into the medical mixture and the ability of the Occupational Medical Practitioner to provide significant data to patients and which, if such information were enabled to be transmitted, would measurably alter medical outcomes as well as enhance and inform the patient's ability to formulate sound medical decisions regarding treatment procedures. Patients assume a certain amount of confidentiality in dealing with physicians in a traditional doctor-patient relationship. In the workers' compensation system, work injury information is not confidential. Communications between physicians and patients are turned into reports that are transmitted to the employer, insurance company, judges and many others involved in the claim (190). However, health care providers should only provide information in their reports relevant to the worker's claim. A treating physician should explain the confidentiality issues to the patient. Undoubtedly, the insurance company requires the most information to process the claim. The employer is to receive periodic reports concerning progress, work restrictions, and follow up appointments. The patient's immediate supervisor needs to know only potential work restrictions because it would not be appropriate or necessary to discuss other aspects of the patient's case not relevant to the work restrictions. Under California Labor code 6412, this information concerning the work injury transmitted between the interested parties, can not be open to public inspection or made public. This medical confidentiality restriction prevents the needed data to determine long term medical outcomes.

Patient Satisfaction Survey

Patient Satisfaction Surveys function as a traditional measurement instrument for evaluation of clinical performance, and have been on the receiving end of both advocacy and criticism in areas that range from accuracy to validity as a tool for evaluative purposes. The hard truth remains, however, as the only mechanism of feedback available to the patient, as means to express individual sentiments and experiences of medical practice and treatment protocols, it continues to be utilized as the gold standard. The patients are asked their level of satisfaction with waiting times, politeness and professionalism of staff, cleanliness, and overall impression. New reporting systems rate individual health care providers, with insurance companies using patient satisfaction data to profile individual physician performance; a form of report card (191). Disagreement exists about which aspects of physician performance to measure. Physicians tend to focus on technical quality, appropriateness of care and patient satisfaction, whereas payers tend to focus on accessibility of care, distribution of resources, and cost (192).

Employer Satisfaction Survey

Traditionally utilized by the marketing industry, the Employer Satisfaction Survey can prove extremely helpful in determining the shortcomings and deficiencies existent in issues concerning policies and procedures, no matter what the industry. One would justifiably be safe to assume that, in cases in which an employer is dissatisfied with the performance of a given clinic or medical provider practice, migration to an alternative medical provider would be the expected course of action. Yet, this is often not the case. The employer might elect to continue utilizing medical services despite a degree of dissatisfaction, whether ill-conceived or not, but will ultimately serve to disrupt the established relationship enjoyed by employer and medical provider. "Happiness is an ephemeral emotion, too fleeting to have an impact," said Judith Bardwick, who teaches at the University of California, San Diego (193). "Happiness is as significant as hunger. Five minutes and three chicken tacos later, he's full. For any company to be successful in today's business environment, it has to continuously change," says Theresa Welbourne Ph.D., an HR professional. To change, you have to convince yourself that you are dissatisfied with something. "If everybody's happy and content with the way things are, your company is going down the tubes." This is the most important reason that satisfaction is a bad barometer of company success. Introspection with critical analysis by the people working in the facility will yield useful information for improvement.

Insurance Company Satisfaction Survey

As an innovative approach to evaluation of performance outcomes, this survey is equipped with voluminous information that can prove immensely useful and invaluable. Questions can be formulated regarding comparisons to other providers in the region in terms of cost and length of treatment modalities dependent on diagnosis rendered. Insurance companies can customarily identify the overutilization of diagnostic studies, rehabilitation procedures and services, and consultations provided by medical professionals as means by which to curb excessive expenditures and wasteful use of the system. Working in this field requires frequent contact with insurance adjusters and the development of a good business relationship which is founded on sound medical scientific principals, rather than on social contacts. Quality may be difficult to define but most people recognize it when they see it.

OTHER PRACTICE PARAMETERS

Percentage of Patient Referrals to Medical Specialists

Under normal circumstances, the percentage of patient referrals to medical specialists should fall within the range of 5 to 15 percent, and can be quite useful as a measurement for assessing quality of care. At one time while employed at a clinic, it was noted that all patients not recovered within a period of six weeks were transferred to the services of an Orthopedist, thus translating into higher costs for the insurers. The underlying concept of this parameter rests in the notion that it is more likely than not that only a small percentage of cases will require surgical procedure, with the balance positively responding to conservative treatment management methodologies. Specialist referral is considered to be inappropriate unless specific indications exist as distinct from any requests advanced by the injured worker. It is appropriate to see a specialist for a consultation from an expert in that particular part of medicine, but it is not appropriate to transfer the entire care to the specialist unless the patient needs a specialized treatment that only that specialist can provide, i.e. surgery, injections, etc.

Percentage of First Aid Cases

First-aid events fall outside the definition of what is considered to be an injury, and thus can measurably cut costs to the employer. Strict guidelines are utilized for determination of what constitutes first aid, with expectation that the medical provider is fully aware of these directives. In order to quality as a first-aid event, the worker must not be seen more than twice, the assumption is made that he or she will return to full duty work capacity, and that no prescription medications are required. Most often, the percentage of first-aid cases appears to vary in a range between 25 and 35 percent; however, specific geographic location tends to alter this figure dependent on regional differences.

Percentage of Patient Referrals to Physical Therapists

The concept and execution of Modified Duty as an alternative to not participating in work-related activities has markedly changed the options available to injured workers, evolving to be the cornerstone of management in the field of Occupational Medicine. In a poll conducted requesting that professional healthcare providers offer their estimates of what percentage of workers should be capable of returning to work in a modified-duty capacity, the majority of respondents stated that figure to be approximately 95 percent, a figure representative of the ability of Modified Duty to indirectly resolve a multiplicity of problems surrounding return-to-work issues, as listed below:

- Elimination of time off as reward for illness.
- Promotion of continuous contact with the workplace, precluding displacement from the team and the ideology and activities of teamwork.
- Statistically proven to hasten recovery time.
- Equipped to potentially achieve resolution for psychosocial issues in a spontaneous manner.
- Recovery is vastly benefited by physical activity.
- Pre-empts the potential for an injured worker to slip through the cracks in the system, aiding in the prevention of job loss and sense of low self-esteem, which ultimately leads to further personal and career difficulties.

The elements listed above are well within the purview and thus control of the medical provider, enabling and serving to promote improvements in the level and degree of quality of care. If each medical provider sought to improve these major areas of medical care delivery, we would no doubt experience marked and dramatic positive results as dividends, the beneficiaries of whom would be not only the patients but the field of Occupational Medicine itself as well. It is noteworthy here that the search for and implementation of innovative methods for improving a system sorely in need of refurbishing will serve to promote the health and well-being of workers, add measurably to the levels of labor productivity, and act as a guide to other stakeholders embedded in the Workers' Compensation system, thus allowing the system overall to improve on a broad-based scale.

Chapter Seven

Ill-Defined Injury and Illness

The following are anonymous excerpts of physician comments in a clinical discussion group concerning psychosocial issues in Workers' Compensation patients, January 2003, at the *Physicians Online* website: (http://www.pol.net.)

—*I am beginning to think that virtually every "difficult" Workers' Comp patient (delayed recovery, chronic unexplained pain, new body parts affected due to "overcompensating," etc.) has major psychosocial issues. I don't mean just "malingering," but significant personality or coping disorders that make recovery under the "medical model" almost impossible. Only behavioral engineering will result in progress. What if I say, "I don't know what is causing your pain, but I think you can function normally?"*

—*I'm beginning to think that chronic pain is an industry that consciously or unconsciously propagates itself by encouraging patients to become unbelievably high-utilizing dependent basket-cases that have no hope of getting better.*

—*The very existence of these patients validates chronic pain specialists as having the unique skill and patience required to maintain these patients on a never-ending series of opioids, anticonvulsants, and whatever else they can think of.*

—*Chronic pain is the new psychiatry, where the lack of need for any objective findings for severe disease and disability creates a blank check for endless utilization.*

—*Both the treating physician and patient [injured worker] are financially incentivized to maintain high utilization and propagate the patient's sense of "injury/entitlement." In the behavioral pain model the "interventional pain" physician is an enabler.*

—*It's a relatively small minority that offer[s] "red flags" for chronic pain refractory to the usual therapies, or prolonged disability well outside the ex-*

pected "guidelines" for recovery. For this group, separating the truly hurting from those who might be gaming the system is as much art as science.

INTRODUCTION

For most workers that have sustained an injury, a close correlation can be found to exist between subjective complaints and objective physical pathology. Since the majority of healthcare practitioners are trained in the treatment of physical pathology, treatment outcomes for these patients are generally considered to be excellent or exceed satisfactory results.

A certain portion of patients, however, present with a significant disparity between the original subjective complaints and objective findings. The patient might, for example, present with a variety of *exaggerated* pain behaviors, such as limping, moaning, groaning, and grimacing, despite their physical examination and tests providing unremarkable conclusions. Physicians are often befuddled that their best efforts to correct a known physical abnormality result in an unsatisfactory outcome for the patient who shows no improvement. Eventually, the physician might become somewhat irritated at the demonstrable lack of improvement in the patient, assigning him or her blame in a lack of motivation to recover.

In cases such as these, many patients are then subjected to a host of repetitive and varied medical treatments and testing procedures, leading at times to side effects and treatment complications. The treatment physician might at this point choose to continue the search for this cryptically derived disease with its accompanying amorphous and ill-defined symptoms in order to identify the root cause of the pain. This line of reasoning is based upon the theory that, if the origin of the complaint can be located or identified, it can then be ameliorated or corrected. Perhaps so, but there is a far more accurate and suitable explanation.

Pain specialists are well aware that the extent of a given patient's set of subjective complaints are more often than not related and inextricably tied to a series or pattern of developmental, social, and cultural factors than with any singular, unified physical pathology (25). Some patients presenting with musculoskeletal pain are in possession of an underlying psychosocial, or non-organically-based disorder, not immediately apparent to an external surveyor, such as the physician (51). The non-organic cause of pain might well derive from what is termed a *simulation disorder*, whereby the patient seeks to act out the role of the invalid or ill individual. Disorders of Simulation are vague and ill defined since, in one way or another, they require the diagnosis of non-illness but in a fashion indicating that the patient displays some degree of intentional control. Furthermore, knowledge of these disorders is incomplete, inadequate, and frequently defined by default (81). Or, the patient might not be aware of the obscure, unconscious processes operating, for instance that of a somatoform disorder. Somatoform is defined as denoting psychogenic symptoms resembling those of physical disease (176), but unintentional.

EMOTIONAL PAIN

Somatization Disorder (7, 8,176) is defined as the conversion of mental states into bodily symptoms and characterized by one who presents with physical complaints and is of the belief they have carpal tunnel syndrome or a herniated disk, for example, yet no physical disease is either present or found through conventionally used diagnostic testing and procedures. Individuals who fit in this category are considered to be problem patients, often preoccupied with pain, numbness, at times extending to extreme complaints of paralysis, with the symptoms causing impairment to both their social and work-related activities, and in severe instances, emotional distress. No objective somatic, organic or physical findings determine the origin of pain, serving to complicate the situation further. The disorder resembles in all ways a physical disorder of some nature. Yet, the patient either has no physical problem, or the *symptoms* in and of them are more marked in the extreme than any disorder discernible through physical examination.

Somatization Disorder can be characterized by a multivariate grouping of symptoms that involve pain, gastrointestinal disturbances, sexual malfunction and pseudoneurological (bizarre nervous system) complaints, any and all of which might have originated prior to age 30, are found to be more common in women, and possess complex medical histories, demonstrable of an endless series of laboratory-based and X-ray studies and testing procedures.

A milder form of this disorder, Somatization (4), might present in the aftermath of a relatively minor injury, following which the individual suffers ongoing and increased levels of symptomatology. No matter the procedures or diagnostic measures taken by the physician, the patient appears to worsen incrementally in levels of pain. It has been observed that somatizing patients often become increasingly passive and dependent, at times assuming the role of victim. A thorough and carefully orchestrated medical history will almost always reveal, in one form or another and as time progresses, that these individuals experienced emotional deprivation during childhood.

Individual perception of disease and disability often develop and progress due to factors bearing little relationship to actual pathology. In our present social climate, one that worships at the door of entitlements, some individuals exhibit expectations that others will provide for their welfare, emotionally and physically. For a certain percentage of individuals, illness becomes a full-time occupation and lifestyle in itself, fulfillment achieved through concerted avoidance of perceived unpleasant activities, such as work-related tasks, while simultaneously being in receipt of excessive attention from family members who then assume the role of caretakers. These patients typically overutilize medical services in a maladaptive and inefficient manner (11, 18), often obtaining care from multiple providers, and shifting capriciously from one treatment provider to another on a regularized basis.

Although almost anyone is certainly capable of "somatizing" under conditions of stress, a percentage of individuals appear to be more prone to this behavioral mode. Factors that have been observed to contribute to individual susceptibility to somatizing behavior (194) can include:

- Childhood abuse or emotional deprivation
- Personal turmoil in adulthood
- Learned behaviors
- Secondary gain
- Cultural factors
- Seeking redress for perceived wrongs
- Personality factors, particularly narcissistic and Borderline

PERSONALITY DISORDER TRAITS

Patients with personality disorders often have a sense of powerlessness in dealing with life problems, and physical symptoms may be a way of expressing their distress. In some environments, pain may be the only way to obtain power, family member support, and financial stability through disability payments. In certain cultures, males are not expected to demonstrate signs of weakness and, conversely, and expectations of females are to demonstrate non-assertive behaviors. Whenever cultural rules preclude or hinder the legitimate expression of emotions, somatizing conduct can serve as an avenue for communication, or much-needed release of inhibited feelings.

Illness Phobia involves excessive and obsessive anxiety that one might develop a disease. In most cases, the individuals experience a trivial or minor work-related injury, consequently attempting to extend their length of treatment due to fears of long-term ramifications as byproducts of the injury, often counter to basic common sense. Despite patient anxieties they can be discharged from treatment, often with the assurance of being eligible to reopen the case should future problems arise over the course of the following five-year period.

Hypochondriacal Behavior constitutes the belief that an individual is *already* possessed of a serious disorder, in contrast to the patient identified with Illness Phobia, wherein the patient is excessively anxious that he or she will *develop* the disorder at some arbitrary future date. When examined in an Occupational Medical clinic, these patients focus excessively on minor bodily signals or commonly-observed findings associated with the injury itself, and are overly distressed by the fallacious belief that these negligible indications are implicative of development and progression of a far more catastrophic illness. Individuals presenting with these types of behaviors are not readily assuaged by physician assurances, their beliefs residing well in the notion that severe disease or illness has been overlooked, misidentified, or simply obfuscated by conventional medical procedures. This scenario further escalates into frequently prolonged treatment, developing and evolving into excessive diagnostic studies and testing procedures, most if not all of which are unnecessary and costly.

Conversion Disorder is characterized by a sensory or motor disorder in the absence of organically- or physically-based indications. These individuals present with limb-based numbness or, in extreme cases, paralysis, speech disturbances, visual impairment often extreme enough to cause blindness, or hearing degradation and often loss, yet no diagnostic or testing measurements signify the origins of such symptomatology. The term *conversion* derives from the psychological theory that mental and emotional stressors are converted into physical or somatic maladies, of which the key distinguishing elements of this disorder include the following:

1. *LaBelle Indifference* — These individuals demonstrate relative non-concern regarding the physical debility, despite presenting with sudden onset of a paralyzed extremity.
2. *Psuedoneurologic Manifestation* — The sensory or motor loss is not associated with or related to any anatomically-based neurological function.

These patients are optimally managed and treated through processes of neurological consultation, in association with psychiatric referrals, and most are not considered to be work-related in nature.

CHRONIC DISABILITY SYNDROMES

The following lists the wide variety of current syndromes that fall within the umbrella category of chronic disabilities.

Chronic Fatigue Syndrome
Fibromyalgia Syndrome
Fibrositis Syndrome
Tension Myositis Syndrome
Myofascial Syndrome
Myofascitis Syndrome
Chronic Pain Syndrome

DEFINITIONS

The above list is comprised of precisely what they imply—syndromes, not disease. And, a syndrome is composed of a grouping or *set* of symptoms occurring in combination, identified as having no known cause or consistent signs or patterns, and associated with no established or known pathological etiology.

A *disease*, in contrast, is defined as an entity with established and recognized causation, consistent pattern of anatomical alteration or transformation, and identifiable grouping of signs and symptomatology.

An *illness* is the subjective symptomatology, either physical or psychological, or both, as perceived by the patient. Occupational stress and excessive anxiety associated with work-related activities are often observed to be one amongst many elements that might contribute to and further precipitate an illness.

Disability is viewed as the legal or social system judgment rendered regarding loss of function based in part on medical assessment and opinion. Dependent upon the particular rating system utilized, disability can be determined through a combination of measurable objective findings in conjunction with subjective factors.

PROBLEM

Those engaged in the field of Occupational Medicine and its associated clinics are increasingly observing patients who present with claims associated with chronic disability disorders and assertions that these maladies are work-related in nature, having been either caused by or exacerbated through normal work-associated activities. In order to be classified as an occupational injury, work-related activity is required to be substantially contributive to causation which, in California, is determined to be 10% work-related. These disorders are chronic, ill-defined, and appear to offer either little or no satisfactory treatment protocols. Disorders of this nature do not often appear to be work-related for a multitude of reasons. Despite their unknown etiology, often with the appearance of having been exacerbated by psychosocial stressors, the associated symptomatology of these syndromes often benefit measurably through physical activity, and along with the lack of scientific evidence as to physical or organic causation provides abundant skepticism as to their ability to disable or encourage dysfunction in workers.

Fibromyalgia and *Myofascial Pain Syndrome* would not in themselves commonly be medically considered sufficient to cause severe or acute disability in relationship to work-related and recreational activities. Nonetheless, the injured worker identified with disorders such as these might possess the perception of illness, which leads to somatic preoccupation and subsequent symptom magnification. The well-intentioned health care practitioner, whether a medical physician, chiropractor, or physical therapist, utilizing means of excessive attention and treatment measures, might inadvertently serve to encourage or enable illness-related behaviors in the patient, precipitous in promoting a further perception of debilitating disability and, ultimately, enhancing the inability to perform work-related activities. The physician-patient relationship thus forms a dynamic that feeds, perhaps unconsciously, into the perception of disability, furthering its cause and encouraging the diminishment of patient function.

It best serves the injured worker to remain both emotionally and physically active and stimulated, oriented toward health-related activity, and continue in job-related functions. Disability derived from myofascial pain and fibromyalgic symptomatology is often neither sufficiently enough acute or severe to cause complete dysfunction, given the often observed well-preserved muscle bulk and strength, satisfactory motion and range abilities, and paucity of correlative objective factors or findings of organic disability demonstrated by the patient. Extreme physically strenuous or repetitive activity might of course necessitate restrictive measures at times, contingent upon severity of patient complaint and expressed discomfort.

Evidence- or empirical-based medicine is predicated on a medical model maintaining that demonstrable *objective evidence* of injury or pathology is required if neuromusculoskeletal conditions are to be diagnosable. In contrast, *symptom-based* models represent a diagnosable condition, despite an absence of demonstrable objective evidence, if soft tissue discomfort is present. Since the latter patients have no objective signs to evaluate, the patient assumes control of the management of the case because therapy becomes dictated by the patient's subjective response to treatment. There are no other parameters to go by.

The use of subjective diagnostic criteria exclusively (symptoms only) as means to define a given pathologic condition often creates circumstances in which the goal of treatment is the palliation of symptoms, rather than pathological cure. Although frequently the case in treatment of upper-extremity disorders, the patient assumes the responsibility for determination of the treatment protocol, often lacking basis in sound and pragmatic scientific and medical bases. For example, a patient presents with numbness and tingling in the fingers of the non major hand with no positive findings on evaluation by physical examination, electro-diagnostic, or laboratory findings. There are no factors in the medical history to suggest a cause. Some health care practitioners may call this carpal tunnel syndrome based on the clinical complaint only and institute long and costly treatment without any scientific basis. The proper course is to categorize the problem as an unknown disorder that is not interfering in the individual's daily life and re-evaluate them periodically. No evidence is present to indicate a disease or disorder at this point. A special burden of responsibility falls on the shoulders of the physician to administer treatment or non-treatment when appropriate.

CAUSATION

In those cases in which the occupational physician has rendered the assessment that the physical requirements of work-related activity have exceeded the physical capacity of the worker with potential to result in injury, it is necessary to straightforwardly state that work is adjudged to be a substantial contributing factor. In California, the Workers' Compensation Appeals Board defines *substantial* to be 10 percent. However, if the medical findings of the physical requirements of the job do not exceed the physiological and structural limitations of the musculotendinous structures, it is justified to state that the workplace is not seen to be a causative factor, popular opinion or prevailing attitudes aside.

An important element for determining the work-related degree or nature of injury is that of discerning the activity the individual was engaged in at the initial onset of symptoms. If the activity performed involves a normally conducted bodily function, such as standing or walking, along with the initial onset of symptomatology, such as chest pain, this is deemed to be not of a work-related nature by the California court system (116). This is because the line has to be drawn somewhere because not everything is work related because the individual happens to be at work. Four basic conditions (190) must be met for a workers' compensation claim to be established:

1. There must be an employment relationship.
2. There must be an injury.

LIBRARY

3. The injury must occur in the course of the employment, i.e., at the time of injury, the employee must have been performing service that grew out of and incidental to the employment.
4. The injury must have been caused by the employment.

Opposed to the acute injury however, is the Cumulative Trauma Disorder which develops, over periods varying from weeks to years, as a result of repeated stresses on a particular body part. The concept is based on a *theory* that each repetition of an activity produces some trauma or wear and tear on the tissues and joints of the body. Perhaps the best known occupational trauma disorder is carpal tunnel syndrome, which is caused by compression of the median nerve within the carpal tunnel of the wrist. This theory has been challenged by many medical authorities, but for the time being, physicians are treating these as work related if the job requires repeated wrist movements. Stating that a problem is work related implies that, with the information currently available, with a reasonable degree of certainty, work activities caused the problem. States may vary in the definition of causation, particularly for cumulative trauma disorders and preexisting conditions (197).

MANAGEMENT

In order to control muskuloskeletal symptomatology, it is key to achieve a balance between mechanical stress and the more debilitating effect of inactivity on the protective musculature. This equilibrium can most often be attained through the processes of aerobic exercise, physical conditioning, and psychosocial support which appear to offer extremely beneficial effects in soft tissue injuries. All such injuries should demonstrate a degree of objective improvement within two weeks, regardless of treatment modality used. In cases in which no improvement has been demonstrated, the case will then require a reevaluation for causation and reassessment of treatment regimen.

In further support of symptomatology not being work-related can be demonstrated when symptoms resolve during periods of rest, indicating that the disturbance is due more to muscle fatigue than underlying disorder. Resolution of symptoms in cases where compensation has been denied is yet another indication that the distress or disturbance might be of a non-pathological nature.

CHRONIC PAIN

Chronic Pain Syndrome consists of both pain and suffering and, not surprisingly, many patients are of the belief that their pain and suffering are punishment for past transgressions. Some individuals are able to identify the event for which they are being punished, while others cannot, yet nonetheless maintain a strong believe that chronic pain and chronic illness only occur when people are deserving of them (69, 71, 87).

Chronic pain does not appear to serve any known scientific or medical purpose, in contrast to acute pain, which is integral to an early bodily defense system as an aid and survival mechanism. Chronic pain is quite different, persisting long after its initial onset, such as in the case of a sprained back or serious infection, in which prolonged pain exists well after recovery (22, 23, 24, 21). Yet, some individuals suffer chronic pain symptomatology in the absence of prior root cause that is self-perceived to be real, unremitting, and can be extremely demoralizing and incite mental depressive disorders. In fact, chronic pain can be of such extreme magnitude as to overwhelm all other debilitating symptoms, leading to a dramatic triadic construct, involving suffering, sleeplessness, and extreme sadness.

Approximately 50 to 80 percent of patients who present with depressive symptoms initially were determined to have physical symptomatology (20), and are less likely to receive an accurate psychiatric diagnosis than those who communicate feelings of depression to their physician. The question can then logically be raised as to whether chronic pain *causes* depression or, conversely, does pain *result from* depression? Current evidence is highly supportive of a bi-directional relationship, in which one informs the other to form a combinatory result. Research, from data from the World Health Organization (34), has demonstrated that patients presenting with chronic pain are four times as likely to develop depressive or anxiety disorders as those who are pain-free.

In a review of the epidemiology of pain and depression as observed in primary care medical environments, Von Korff and Simon (195) concluded the following:

1. Pain is strongly associated with anxiety and depression.
2. The number of pain sites and the extent to which pain interferes in daily life are characteristics most strongly predictive of depression.
3. Psychological symptoms of depression, including low energy levels, sleep disturbances, and worry, are commonly experienced symptoms amongst patients, whereas guilt and loneliness are not.

4. Psychological distress often surfaces, then resolves early on in the course
   of a pain disorder that evolves into chronic conditions.

Based on these findings, it would appear that pain and psychological illness
are inherently possessed of reciprocity, constructing a two-pronged cause-
and-effect relationship. The co-morbidity construct of pain-depression are
supported by the following two theories:

1. Some individuals are susceptible genetically to both physical and psychological symptoms, as well as a state in which psychological distress works
   to amplify unpleasant physical discomfort and sensations.
2. The physical discomfort and stress related to pain can induce psychological distress, as the two work in cohesion to intensify the effects of each.

Persistent pain is characterized by more intense sensitivity to pain, decreased threshold levels to painful stimuli, and episodic spontaneous occurrence of pain. Individuals who present with persistent pain complaints also
often display unresponsiveness to what is considered normal painful stimuli,
as well as experiencing painful reactions to normally painless stimuli. Many
of these symptoms appear to result from alterations or anomalies in the central nervous system, resulting in sensitization and desensitization contingent
upon the stimuli applied (38).

Clinical trials have demonstrated that antidepressants can provide quite effective pain relief within the framework of a clinical setting. Patients administered antidepressants are four times more likely to report overall improvement in symptoms than those receiving placebo. The antidepressant group
reports improvements in sleep patterns, fatigue levels, pain episodes, and
general well-being.

Co-morbidity rates of pain and depression might be infinitely more difficult to treat than depression alone. Pain can perpetuate the depression,
whereas depression might well perpetuate the pain; again, evidence of a re-
ciprocal, co-dependent pattern relationship. This obstinate and difficult to
manage syndrome might best be served through an integrated, interdisciplinary approach to treatment, including but not limited to use of medication,
physical therapy, and behavioral and psychological-based therapies.

The posture of therapeutic activism that states, "Don't just stand there, do
something!" finds its place among practices of medicine as well, yet does not
acquit itself well in the management of chronic pain when in the absence of
physically-based disease. This medical conundrum might best profit from in-
verting that phrase to heed the injunction, "Don't just do something, stand
there" (Szasz, 1975), based on medical observation that, frequently, the more

the use of diagnostic studies and treatment, the worse the condition of the patient. In a majority of these cases, the patient might well be better managed and be more likely to achieve positive results if ministered to by pain management specialists than those in the clinical setting of Occupational medicine.

Even when performing at its optimum level, the Workers' Compensation system produces its share of injured workers who de-compensate, develop problems of dysfunction, and ultimately progress to become chronic pain patients. In the event of a work-related injury, the worker might begin to experience a diminished sense of self, feeling demeaned and unwanted should the employer not request the individual's return to work, or in cases in which co-workers become critical of his or her arrangement of modified duty. The importance, therefore, of returning the injured worker to his or her former job as expeditiously as is possible cannot be overemphasized. It is widely accepted knowledge that the probability of returning to work decreases proportionately to the longer the time away from the job. These are factors that must, of necessity, be considered thoroughly prior to establishing diagnosis and setting up treatment protocols, and further demanding strict adherence to a predetermined schedule with mutually agreed-upon objectives between the treatment physician and worker.

THE SECONDARY INJURY

Another frequently encountered issue consists of cases in which the worker communicates discomfort deriving from a secondary injury as an offshoot of the original, resulting from the accommodation or compensation for the prior-injured upper limb. In compensating for or accommodating the one, originally-injured extremity, the patient will overutilize the other, causing fatigue to its structure through excessive, repetitive strain and/or overuse. There does not appear to be medical basis for such conclusion considering that, if such were the case, amputees would be in a state of unrelenting suffering due to overuse syndrome. It does appear, however, to be a product of patient imaginings and excessive suggestibility through peer pressure. There is, of course, understandable muscle soreness from the increased use not normally experienced by the patient. The resolution to such complaints and discomfort is concentration on appropriate repair of originally-induced problem, with return to normal use of the injured part as the primary objective. The patient is optimally benefited by not being permitted to advance the cause of his or her complaints further with additional claims and treatment protocols. The treatment provider thus must consider all aspects of a patient's presenting complaints and discomforts, taking under advisement each phase of patient progress and evaluating, and if necessary reevaluating, the patient as a whole in a sometimes ever-changing dynamic. If the injury is viewed with the perspective that not only is the physical being of the patient at risk, but the mental and emotional as well, the treatment options will broaden and become more fluid, allowing the physician to approach the patient in a more flexible manner. Should secondary injuries emerge during the course of treatment, by rechanneling the focus to the original injury, in a sense diverting the patient's attention away from the secondary disturbance, the opportunity for hastening the process of recovery will be all the greater, with the ultimate result that of a fully functional return-to-work status.

As so eloquently stated by Justice Louis Brandeis:

The duty of a lawyer today is not that of a solver of a legal conundrum; he is indeed a counselor of law. Knowledge of the law is of course essential to his efficiency, but the law bears to his profession a relation very similar to that which medicine does to that of the physicians. . . . It requires but a mediocre physician to administer the proper drug for the patient who correctly and fully describes his ailment. The great physicians are those who in addition to that knowledge of therapeutics which is open to all, knows not merely the human body but the human mind and emotions, so as to make the proper diagnosis—to know the truth which their patients fail to disclose and who add to this an influence over the patient which is apt to spring from a real understanding of him. (143)

Chapter Eight

Disorders of Simulation

The good ended happily, and the bad unhappily.
This is what fiction means.

—Oscar Wilde, *1895*

MALINGERING

Malingering is considered by many to be a predominant cause of insurance fraud, estimated to range from 1 to 3 percent of all filed claims. Although small in percentage, the overall high claim rate causes it to be a major as well as costly problem. Although considered by some to be largely comprised of myth due to its low annual rate of successful prosecution, others believe it to be of prime concern, with the two groups directly polarized at opposite ends of the spectrum.

The 1993 "Little Hoover Commission" Report (1), based on an investigation conducted in California, concluded that 30 percent of systems costs, or $3 billion per year, is expended wastefully on fraudulent activity (2), with 20 to 30 percent of employee claims considered fraudulent in nature, and businesses twice as likely as injured workers to commit fraud (3). Despite these figures, the claims have not been fully substantiated. The California Applicants' Attorneys' Association refers to 1998 statistics that indicate 358 fraud arrests, three-quarters of which included injured workers, amounting to less than one-tenth of one percent of total claims filed.The incidence of prosecutions in these cases can more be related to the difficulty encountered in substantiating and corroborating these activities than in its low rate of prevalence.

Claimant fraud is more easily detectable, and more amenable to investigation and prosecution than that of employer or insurance fraud, occurring even in legitimate injury cases, in which injured workers fabricate events in order to obtain additional benefits. Employers and insurers are apt to hold to the belief that one of the many functions and objective goals of anti-fraud programs includes the deterrence of such ill-advised conduct, with punishment ensuing should it occur. A large number of injured workers, along with their attorneys, vociferously proclaim the program's inequity in its tendency to create a public persona of the injured worker as being in the business of swindling the system for self-benefit and reward. This group further claims that, in light of the anti-fraud program receiving its funding from employers, it is inherently biased against the injured worker.

In a 1997 survey conducted by the *Coalition against Insurance Fraud*, 21 percent of respondents indicated that perpetrators should receive either little or no punishment based on their perception that the insurance industry is at fault for the unethical behavior of individuals.

It is safe to state that overall public attitude is a crucial factor in the curtailment of fraud, with tolerance and entitlement philosophies both driving and contributing to an atmosphere that more easily rationalizes defrauding the system with impunity and little or no social stigma attaching to this unethical behavior pattern. The general public should have at its disposal all information necessary to forge and bolster the conviction that fraud is a major contributor to the steep rise in rates of insurance premiums, and that insurers are diligently working to both detect and deter fraud utilizing preemptive measures and policies.

In practical terms, is it possible to construct a viable profile of the malingerer? Based on statements owing to Freud's hypothesis, a normal individual is characterized as one who is both able to love and work (82), while inferring that the malingerer who demonstrates no desire to work is mentally ill. In more traditional terms, malingering is defined as little more than immoral behavior, or the intentional, voluntary production, exaggeration, or false attribution of symptoms that simulate a physical or mental disorder, usually inåvolving external or secondary gain, or external incentives, such as that of avoidance of work or military duty, financial compensation, the evasion of criminal prosecution, or drug procurement (DSM-IV–TR, fourth edition, APA, 2000). A majority of individuals who fit the profile of malingerer often suffer from a variety of personality disorders (199,200).

An injury, accident, or illness serve the purposes well of any given personality disorder in its ability to nourish the underlying psychopathology. Both Paranoid Personality and Borderline Personality Disorder possess as their common thread the element of vocational stress, often converting itself into a declared inability to work on the part of the patient. Further, these disorders include in their repertoire of symptomatology an enhanced perception of both pain and anxiety, often subordinate or secondary to the traditional concomitant pain associated with severe physical or mental limitations.

Patients suffering from psychosocial stressors also present with qualities of impaired pain tolerance, experiencing functional difficulties in normal course of daily living activities. It is not uncommon to observe incidences of failing marriages often preceding work-related injuries of chronic pain disorders, or extensive and complicating pain limitations resulting from minor accidents. Registered complaints that directly relate to the injury might offer the claimant non-work status eligibility, thus providing more time at home in order to attempt to salvage a disintegrating relationship.

Psychological stressors can include strained relationships and dysfunctional familial support systems, economic vulnerabilities and weaknesses, and possibly legal-related issues.

Malingerers often reveal a history of drug abuse, disrespect for the rights and property of others, erratic employment records, conflicts with the law, marital difficulties, impulse and anger management control issues, a chaotic early childhood, juvenile delinquency, and depression and anxiety disorders; behaviors that might well elicit the moral condemnation of health care deliverers.

Health professionals are taught that all patients must be afforded expert diagnosis and treatment, and the failure to acknowledge the existence of illness prevarication might serve to protect health caregivers from the often-distasteful emotional experience of outrage and confrontation. The treatment of all patient symptomatology, without benefit of investigation, often provides the healthcare professional a facile method for extricating oneself from the rigors of further examination. Those engaged in the healthcare professions are taught to assume the role of patient advocacy, thus enabling and aiding the malingerer toward successful deceptive behaviors.

Several professionals are of the belief that the diagnosis of malingering deserves little if any role in the field of medicine, predicated on the premise that physicians are not trained in the fields of social and/or legal issues, and thus are not equipped to level such judgments (Szasz, 1956). Reluctance on the part of physicians to diagnose an individual as a malingerer is thus quite understandable; however, the clinician is always at the mercy of engaging in speculative reasoning, second-guessing logic, and the assessment of patient intentions. To state it another way, the task is not simply one of medical assessment, but rather involves the ability to judge the far-reaching impact that might result from a given patient's social problems, a process that can often place undue strain on the inherent trust traditionally enjoyed by the doctor-patient relationship. Nonetheless, it is the responsibility of any Occupational

Medicine Practitioner to appropriately evaluate and assess the patient's difficulties, provide sufficient treatment methods and, of course, do no harm.

Defined as "the intentional production of false or exaggerated symptoms
motivated by external incentives" (APA, 1994), malingering involves the following four characteristics, all of which comprise its parameters, and for
which a brief discussion of each will follow:

1. An unexplainable symptom.
2. Intentional actions.
3. An understandable goal.
4. A cost-effective solution (monetary compensation).

An Unexplainable Symptom

A given patient presenting with unexplained symptomatology can be defined
as in danger of being assessed as a malingerer, albeit the boundary lines are
somewhat narrow yet surprisingly complex in nature. Generally, the complaints voiced by malingerers are often disproportionate relative to the results
of the physical examination. The primary flaw of the imposter is overacting.
The patient medical history is anomalous to the present symptomatology; the
lab values are incorrect, and the physical signs are not evident. The customary cause-and-effect relationship often observed between a medical event and
its symptomatology is often grossly exaggerated in cases of malingering. Further, it is not uncommon for individuals to alter their descriptions of events,
describing their symptoms in dramatically varied ways over the course of
time. Careful investigation and examination of this convoluted path will usually betray the symptom to be external to the bounds of medical science.

Intentional Actions

In that it is a subjective assessment of the medical provider in any event, understanding the intentions of a patient is of limited importance in asserting
an accurate diagnosis. This is fortunate because it is difficult to determine
whether the acts of an individual are intentional or not. Many times it is as
difficult to demonstrate intent in the clinic as it is to prove fraud in the
courtroom. The medical practitioner relies on the presumption that an individual's behavior is under his or her control, excluding cases in which the
patient has been determined to possess an underlying psychiatric disorder
which restricts voluntary behavior (like compulsions, phobias, and psy-
chosis). For example, the individual with a hair pulling compulsion intentionally carries out his act, but he does not do it voluntarily because he can

not refrain from doing it. The involuntary nature of the act categorizes his behavior to psychopathology (201).

An Understandable Goal

Those classified as malingerers hold to the perspective that their problems might best be effectively resolved through resolution of their suffering if based upon medical or psychiatric disorder and, as a result, they seek the endorsement and substantiation of medical professionals. Thus, as medical professionals we are then confronted with the dilemma of determining whether the individual intends to solve the problem through symptomatology, the first step of which is to ascertain whether the patient's problem conforms to the definition of an *understandable goal*. The second step consists of the establishment of an existing social problem that might sufficiently complete the characteristic profile of malingering.

The patient need not verbally confess his or her goal in order for the medical practitioner to formulate a diagnosis. Any medical practitioner faced with a patient who argues vociferously in favor of the cause of his or her symptoms, while displaying resistance to or overtly rejecting obvious medical solutions and outrage at the clinician's attempts at reassurance, would be logically hard-pressed to conclude a diagnosis other than malingering.

Cost-Effective Solution

The malingerer's presenting symptoms must consist of a reasonable cost for the anticipated payoff. In cases where the symptoms provide costly resolution, yet the payoff is sizable, as in cases of litigation, the diagnosis of malingering can still be determined based upon an understandable cost/benefit ratio.

Diagnosis

One must be mindful that the malingerer is engaging in a form of medical charade and that, in order to formulate this diagnosis, all the elaborate components of the puzzle must fit together—an unexplained symptom, intentional actions, an understandable goal, and cost-effective solution. Through careful review of these distinct issues, the clinician should soon discover the diagnosis to often emerge with surprising clarity. The clues might surface through the use of interview, historical investigation or the very path traversed by the patient. Katz (202) asserts that some complex mysteries based in law can be resolved through review of the path of events.

A checklist that reviews the path of events, the Barkemeyer-Callon-Jones Malingering Detection Scale, incorporated within it the activities and behaviors of the malingerer, is a useful instrument for the detection of this disorder [refer to Attachment B(14)].

COMPENSATION NEUROSIS

Compensation Neurosis can be defined as the perpetuation of a disabling condition, at least partially under volitional control, and often resolving coincidentally with termination of the legal process, and considered to be an *unconscious*, genuinely disabling and compensable condition. Imagine, if you will, the speculative situation in which $200 has been set aside for an individual in the event of need, with the proviso that these funds not be used unless deemed necessary. How much time will pass, we conjecture, before human nature rears up in certain individuals faced with this hypothetical situation, forcefully dictating their need for the use of the funds where no perceptible need in fact exists? Our unconscious minds will thus direct our behavior in order to achieve a perceived benefit, our symptoms thus continuing until such time as we are in receipt of that desired benefit.

Secondary gain refers to an unconscious protraction of a disorder in order to obtain both benefit and satisfaction. The Index of the *DSM-III-R*, under the section titled "Psychological Factors Affecting Physical Condition" defines Compensation Neurosis. The processes of the conscious and unconscious mind are certainly useful and interesting concepts relating to discussions of mental disorders yet can prove enormously problematic when constructing an analysis of simulation disorder. Insurmountable difficulties can occur in cases in which physical and emotional behaviors have been observed to be the result of implied or inferred activities. These activities are, by virtue of their cause, intangible elements, difficult to observably discern.

What can be viewed as more useful is the determination of *intention* and *volition*, whereby intention suggests the planning, engineering, and/or design of an activity. The planning of such behavioral activities might be quite simple in its construct, for example, offering the equivocal response "I don't know" to a majority of the medical examiner's questions. Purposeful behavior such as this clearly denotes a form of intentional avoidance of questioning in an indirect manner (81), serving to arouse the suspicions of the medical examiner.

When engaged in what is termed *voluntary* behavior, patients demonstrate control of their presentation. For example, a patient might choose to display evidence of symptoms at one moment's interval, while camouflaging signs of illness or injury in the next, contingent upon an assessment of the situation. Thus, patients classified as having Compensation Neurosis both display a lack of intention yet their behavior is considered to be voluntary in nature. This paradox is explained by the observation that after an injury, these patients become hypochondriacal if they have persistent symptoms or believe they suffered permanent damage. Oftentimes, they say someone is going to pay for this and make no effort to recover until the extent of the injury has been evaluated. During this period of self-observation the patient develops an attitude of introspection which increases with time and requires reeducation before rehabilitation can be accomplished (203). The hope of a large settlement or disability benefit appears to act as an unconscious motive. Determining the distinction between deliberate exaggeration, self-suggestion, selective perception, and other mechanisms contributing to this reaction is very difficult (204).

FACTITIOUS DISORDERS

Factitious Disorder is defined as the *intentional, involuntary* compulsive production of symptoms in order to simulate a physical or psychological disorder, existing exclusively to both assume and maintain the role of "patient." Intentional refers to the intentional production of symptoms in order to receive attention. However, the actions do not appear to be under voluntary control because of an underlying psychological disorder, and the patient is not malingering (205). This disorder in all likelihood requires a quite disturbed mentally dysfunctional state, such as observed in Borderline Personality Disorder, particularly in that not only might such individuals report a nonexistent injury, but also possess the capacity to inflict painful, genuine injury or disease to themselves as well as others.

The *malingerer* desires the *appearance* of sickness, while the patient identified with *factitious disorder* desires to *be* ill. Any self-induced disorder has the potential to evolve to that of factitiousness, however, the course the disorder assumes over time is equally as important as its root cause. Those patients injured in an accident can also be classified with factitious disorder if their subsequent behavior embraces the sick role, whether by actively maintaining the disabling condition or through passive avoidance of treatment protocols and medication. While the malingerer can engage in work- and leisure-related activities when he or she perceives oneself to not be observed, those classified with factitious disorder will remain in a state of disability in ways that defy sensibility and are extremely costly in nature.

Sociologist Talcott Parsons first described the function of the "sick role" in society (1951), noting that sickness and/or injury accords noticeable benefit and obligation (124). A sick individual is neither held accountable or responsible for the condition, and is additionally the beneficiary of the noticeable attention and concern of others. Some of these benefits might include respite from work-, family, social-, and sexual-related obligations. Certain behaviors are expected of the informed individual, some of which include the concept that the illness is an undesirable state and there exists an innate obligation to seek the assistance of medical professionals, in addition to full participation and cooperation in the process of recovery.

It can be considered a near-impossible task for a medical practitioner to provide reassurance to hypochondriacal patients due to their overvaluation of the concept of bodily dysfunction. The Healthcare Provider might, for instance, schedule yet another testing procedure, in the hope of reassuring the patient, yet the patient persists in an undeniable obsessive preoccupation of his or her symptoms. Patients might well demonstrate the *appearance* of participation in the recovery process, yet will nonetheless expend immeasurable energy in securing ever-greater quantities of attention, a deceptive practice that can easily disarm the non-vigilant or unaware clinician who justifiably expects cooperation where none exists. Further, these patients might be found to exhaust vast levels of energy within the health care system, while typically offering no participatory involvement in the restorative process, thus nullifying all efforts at potential successful recovery.

Hypochondriasis is considered a subset of somatoform disorder in which, unlike those patients identified with factitious disorder, these individuals do not seek to maintain the role of patient. Rather, the hypochondriac is not cognizant of the operational underlying psychological factors in the genesis of this disorder. In contrast, much like the factitious patient, the malingerer consciously constructs symptomatology, with the objective goal often residing in financial benefit, not in the maintenance of the role of patient.

The preceding chapter serves the purpose of outlining the multivariable disorders that contribute to fraudulent behaviors and practices observed in the Workers' Compensation system. As medical professionals, the best line of defense is to equip oneself well with the sizable data available on the genesis and characteristics of these disorders in order to optimally and most effectively diagnose patients as malingerers when appropriate. Understanding the root cause of these disorders can offer responsible, valid, and formidable leverage when dealing with the deceptive behaviors owing to the established profile and parameters of a malingerer, thus enabling the medical practitioner to improve his or her diagnostic abilities and gain greater success in so doing.

Chapter Nine

Management of the Difficult Patient

Three Golden Rules for Malingering:
  1. You must make the impression you hate to be ill.
  2. Make up your mind for one disease and stick to it.
  3. Don't tell the doctor too much.

—Richard Asher, 1945

BACKGROUND

Comprising 5 to 15 percent of total Workers' Compensation patients, difficult patients are characterized by the primary manner in which they conduct themselves and interact with the healthcare provider, frequently demonstrating distrust, manipulative behavior, are excessive demanding, noncompliant, with an often marked inability to improve medically. Those seeking a high level of nonproductive medical care as means to validate compensation claims can be identified as malingerers as well (10).

Clinicians often experience a sense of demoralization when treating such patients, owing to an unending array of physical concerns, the inability to achieve a satisfactory level of cure, and complaints that sufficient enough efforts are not being carried out, all of which can serve to instill doubt in the physician, causing him or her to feel emotionally drained and physically exhausted (99). These frustrating and seemingly hostile patients frequently evoke strong negative reactions in medical practitioners, stemming for the most part from the inability to establish and maintain an effective physician-patient relationship (1, 2), which is the bulwark of effective and satisfactory medical care. The establishment of rapport between doctor and patient is imperative to the ideal medical relationship, serving to formulate a partnership with the common goal of solving the medical puzzle, doctor and patient working in combination. Traditional medical training places great emphasis on the detection of physical disease in a manner not unlike the deconstruction of a murder mystery. Intellectual satisfaction, often gained from searching out, detecting, and solving difficult-to-diagnose diseases owing to the requirements of problem-solving ability, often proves immensely challenging in nature. Yet, symptomatological cause for certain patients is never discovered, with dramatic and marked differences in perception often noted between physician and patient as to the level and gravity of the illness and degree of disability (3). Often resulting from the inexplicable symptoms, patients often sense a lack of empathy and understanding from the physician, in turn causing the physician to question the validity and look skeptically upon the compensation claim.

The optimal manner in which to approach complicated patients with unexplained symptoms can include several significant stages, the first of which is to clarify the differences between illness and disease (9), first characterized by Fabrega in 1978 (206). Disease has at its root pathological origin, whereas illness is the perception of feeling abnormal or sick. Although many patients might present with disease and illness in combination, several others might possess disease without illness, and others illness without disease present (5). For example, patients with an undiagnosed asymptomatic disease are not ill; people who are grieving or worried may feel ill but have not disease. Patients and doctors who recognize this distinction and who realize how common it is to feel ill and have no disease are less likely to search needlessly for disease pathology. If physical disease can be eliminated as causative to symptomatology, one can then concentrate on those disorders that are characterized by the manifestation and exhibition of symptoms exclusively.

The disorders that stem from illness without the presence of disease might be further categorized in relation to whether or not a disorder of simulation is present. In that the management of simulation disorders differs substantially from that of traditional disease and illness, it is mandatory that accurate diagnosis be determined for simulation disorders, which include malingering, factitious disorders, and compensation neurosis.

Personality disorder can be described as a marked aberration in thought processes or emotional bases causing the individual difficulty in interaction and communication with others as well as inability to adapt to the surrounding environment.

MALINGERING

The following lists the diagnostic criteria for malingering (73, 76, 80, 81, and 84):

1. Exaggerated, misattributed, or false symptoms.
2. Causation might be fabricated.
3. Detection of false symptom reporting.
4. The ability to control and produce symptoms at will, electing to simulate and express symptoms at the most opportune and prudent times.
5. Hostility toward others, utilizing circumvention techniques, such as non-responsive mechanisms or evasion of questions.
6. Remaining in treatment as long as a way to manipulate the system is detected.
7. Abnormal or aberrant interpersonal relationships, including forming poor working relationships with clinicians, low-level frustration tolerance, unsatisfactory and low degree of interpersonal conflict resolution ability.
8. Personality Pathology, exhibiting or more of the following behavioral traits:
   a. Sadistic
   b. Antisocial
   c. Narcissistic
   d. Passive-Aggressive
   e. Borderline
   f. Compulsive

The diagnostic criteria formulated for malingering do not, in themselves, offer absolute certainty for diagnosing this disorder, owing to their lack of ability to distinguish between the "distorting influences," exhibited by certain ill patients, and the act of "deliberate deception." The unintentional distortion of verbal expression or behavior is commonly evidenced in ill patients, thus must be excluded prior to concluding that malingering might be present. Evaluation anxiety, general fatigue, limited intelligence, inattention, memory deficits, and mental disorders can all contribute to unintentional disorders in ill patients. The failure to account for these contributory factors will no doubt render invalid any conclusions reached by a medical practitioner regarding malingering.

Any magnification of symptoms by a given patient can be considered a form of escape from perceived irresolvable conflict as means to provide opportunity for gain or to ensure the maintenance of the role of patient.

Overall, clinicians demonstrate poor performance in the detection of malingering when using available information that derives exclusively from the patient (15). However, accuracy rises measurably if malingering is considered to be a component part of the differential diagnosis (which one of two or more diseases or conditions the patient is suffering from by systematically comparing their clinical findings). Detection of malingering can prove difficult owing to the individual's feigning a physical disorder by expressing genuine levels of distress often owing to their current life circumstance, and the subsequent displacement of that stress to an alternative cause or element. False imputation is often created through a process of equating genuine distress with symptom presentation rather than an occult or unrevealed psychosocial problem.

The possibility exists for any physical or mental disorder to either be feigned or exaggerated, and thus those factors considered important to the detection of deception include:

• Inconsistency in medical history or examination.
• Improbability that set of symptoms is medically plausible.
• Understanding of the patient's current situation, both personal and social.
• Emotional reactions to the symptoms, i.e., reporting severe distress, while appearing comfortable.
• Consistency using standardized assessment measures:
• Tests usually performed and interpreted by psychologists such as the Patient Pain Profile (by C. David Tollison and Jerry C. Langley) and the Validity Indicator Profile (by Richard I. Frederick, PhD) assessments.
• Tests for simulation:
  The Barkemeyer-Callon-Jones Malingering Detecting Scale,
  The Test of Memory Malingering, and
  The Minnesota Multiphasic Inventory-2.

A medical history evaluation will likely provide the most valuable resource in attempting to detect malingering disorder, with two areas to examine to include what can be gleaned external to that which the patient reports, and what can be gathered during patient interview. Information derived from corroborative sources is extremely important, obtained through careful review of medical records, employment background, and interviews with family, friends, and/or employers.

Several clues that can be obtained that might possibly be indicative of deception include:

• Blatant rather than subtle description of symptoms.
• An improbable number of symptoms, with extreme severity.
• Many rare symptoms.
• Either an unusually sudden onset or resolution of symptomatology that appears to be implausible, given the nature of the disorder.
• Demonstration of substantial impairment considered inconsistent with the disorder.
• Marked incongruities that exist between actual presentation of patient symptoms and reported impairment.

- Theatrical or histrionic quality to symptom presentation.
- Difficulty in recollecting actual symptoms reported and level of severity.
- Improbable or absurd symptoms.
- Excessively specific symptom description in combination with unrealistic precision.
- Symptom combinations unlikely to medically coexist.

In attempting to accurately discern and detect deceptive behavior, the medical practitioner can be served well by the fact that most fakers are often seen to provide a lay concept of impairment associated with the disorder, frequently in direct discordance with actual features of the illness or disease. A thorough knowledge of what should be expected in dealing with a specific disorder is a required facet for ascertaining such discrepancies. It is safe to assume that any given individual is capable of acquiring textbook knowledge of the general symptomatology associated with a disorder, subsequently offering a verbal recitation of these characteristic symptoms to a medical examiner. The experienced clinician, nonetheless, should thus be sufficiently equipped to perceive these anomalies or irregularities in the patient's presentation.

Through the use of physical examination, Waddell (52, 56) separated the standard signs of physical pathology from that of the inappropriate signs of illness behavior. The most commonly-observed feature of all inappropriate signs includes that of magnification, termed "magnified illness behavior." In the absence of distress, fear, mistaken belief system, and/or inadequate coping mechanisms, it appears more likely than not that these signs are indicative of simulation disorder.

An organic or physiologically-based disorder is not grounds for the exclusion of malingering and, conversely, the presence of malingering disorder is not the basis for excluding an organic disorder. Therefore, the clinician must possess the ability and awareness to distinguish between unintentional distortion and deliberate or intentionally deceptive behavior, and be capable of recognizing the wide range of circumstances within which distortion and deception might occur.

FURTHER CLUES TO MALINGERING

1. The claimed injuries do not match or parallel the minor nature of the accident, a classic example of which is the soft tissue injury that follows a low-velocity car crash.

2. Medical record inconsistencies, such as incorrect demographic information, shifting descriptions of the injuries over time.
3. In cases in which one or more patients present a post office box number or hotel address rather than a street address.
4. The patient might appear to be overly directing the treatment plan or protocol by requesting specific drugs, treatment modalities, or therapeutic services.
5. The patient might transfer to alternative physicians at a time that coincides directly with issuance of a release for work.
6. The patient displays excessive neediness, demanding large quantities of attention from the healthcare providers.
7. The patient possesses prior history of drug abuse, with demonstration of drug-seeking behavior.
8. Another treating physician has established a pattern of overtreatment of patient.
9. Patient failure to return to work after being informed of release from medical treatment.
10. Treatment for injury initiated more than three weeks following accident occurrence.
11. Attending physician treats patient for problems that fall outside the scope of his or her medical practice.

Underestimation of both the knowledge and skill of the malingerers is commonly encountered amongst physicians. These individuals might be capable of gaining access to textbooks that describe in-depth medical disorders and their accompanying physical examination procedures, including methodology used in the detection of symptom falsification. Medical libraries are open to the general public, allowing for ease of use for any intelligent individual to locate and obtain information related to a given medical condition, in addition to the expansive quantity of available data on the Internet.

The patient who suffers an injury (55) might later be found to magnify or feign continuing medical difficulties. Extensive contact with lawyers, doctors, and other patients provide the patient a superb training ground for learning the symptomatology of the genuine disorder.

In relation to sensory nerve injuries, both the public and at times even many physicians anticipate pain as the primary presenting symptom. Yet, in reality, reduced or decreasing levels of pain are encountered more often than not following injury, resulting in numbness not pain one week post-injury.

The electro-diagnostic studies, such as the electro-myogram and nerve conduction velocity test will not prove positive until indication of advanced degeneration is present, customarily after three weeks' time, in motor nerve injuries. Irritation that precedes degeneration causes muscle spasm and, as the degeneration progresses, weakness and ultimately muscle atrophy occurs, which can prove to be valuable clues and lend support to those clinicians in conducting a physical examination. Circumferential measurements of extremities, along with opposite side comparison, also prove indispensable in evaluation of motor nerve injury.

NON-ORGANIC SIGNS

The findings derived from physical examination will provide signs of organically-based problems, indicating the presence of either pathology or disease. In contrast, signs of non-organic problems include those findings that are considered normal presentation of a specific disorder. Both organic and non-organic signs might be present in patients describing low back pain, and thus it is best to not equate the presence of non-organic signs alone as indicative of malingering disorder, or the presence of psychological behavioral problems, instead viewed as the need for further investigation and evaluation.

A group of signs, indicating the presence of non-organic problems for a group of patients presenting with low back pain, was described by Waddell (56, 57, 58, 59, 61), who referred to these indicators as "behavioral" or "inappropriate" signs. The testing procedures for these signs can be conducted in less than one minute as part of the normal physical examination. The inadequate administration or misapplication of these signs in the past caused controversy regarding their efficacy.

During the early part of the 1900s, non-organic signs were frequently used to detect malingering amongst those patients with low back pain (53), however, as medical and psychological knowledge developed and progressed, it became clear that the diagnosis for malingering might have been more based on overly simplistic assumptions, and thus non-organic signs as indicators for malingering encountered decreasing popularity.

From 1980 to the present, non-organic signs have increased in use following Waddell's studies as a means to confirm their effectiveness in confirming low back pain, through his grouping of eight signs into five categories when performing physical evaluation, as described below:

1. Tenderness
   * Skin tenderness upon light palpation does not follow normal anatomical boundaries. Physical low back pain is usually localized, not causing tenderness upon light touch.

2. Simulation
   - Axial Loading—pressing down on top of the head should not produce low back pain.
   - Simulated Rotation—when rotating the shoulders and pelvis in unison, the back structures are not stressed. If the patient reports pain during this maneuver, the test is considered to be positive.
3. Distraction
   - The distracted straight-leg raise test—the supine straight leg-raising test should coincide with extension of the knee while in the sitting position. If this does not occur, the test result is positive.
4. Regionalization
   - If the patient describes either a stocking or glove distribution of numbness or one that involves an entire extremity or one side of the body, the result is positive.
   - A cogwheel effect occurs in muscle testing for regional weakness can be determined as positive. When true muscle weakness is present, the muscle is smoothly overpowered with no jerking movement.
5. Overreaction
   - Exaggerated response to stimulus—positive signs include disproportionate grimaces, tremors, sweating, or collapse.

Waddell concluded that the presence of three or more of these signs correlates with results of the administration of psychological tests that indicate a problem with the case. Clinicians should consider whether overutilization of treatments exists when patients fall within this category and no progress has been recorded. It might better serve these patients to have their treatment more focused on addressing the illness behavior itself.

A physical problem might coexist as well with the presence of non-organic signs, thus we can assume that the presence of non-organic signs does not in itself eliminate the need for further and more exhaustive physical examination. Non-organic signs alone cannot be equated with malingering or even the presence of psychological disorders. Rather, these types of behavioral signs should alert the physician to a need for further and more comprehensive testing procedures. In testing for non-organic signs related to musculoskeletal disorders present in regions of the body other than the back are not commonly used, thus development of such indicators might serve in guiding management of these patients.

The most important psychological disturbance is that of emotional distress in patients presenting with chronic low back pain, further defined through these use of questionnaires as an increased bodily awareness and depression. Psychological distress associated with low back pain presents clinically in the form of inappropriate descriptions of symptoms and irregularities in response to physical examination. It has been recognized that further tests might prove useful for discerning the myriad causative factors resident in these responses, descriptions of which follow.

OTHER USEFUL TESTS IN THE PHYSICAL EXAMINATION

Mankopf's Test—Pain increases pulse rate, therefore palpation of painful area or areas should likewise demonstrate an increase in pulse rate by 5 percent or more.

O'Donoghue's Maneuver—In patients with true physiological pain, the passive range of motion proves to be greater than active range of motion. However, a positive behavioral sign can be concluded should a greater degree of active range of motion result.

McBride's Test—Request that the patient stand on one leg while raising the opposite knee toward the chest area, a position that should decrease lower back pain, with an increase in pain indicative of a positive behavioral sign.

Hoover's Test—Place the patient in a supine position. While holding the patient's heels off the table, ask the patient to raise one leg. The test proves negative if the leg is raised up with ease, and positive if the patient reports an inability to raise one leg, with no downward pressure being exerted on the contralateral leg (54).

Burn's Test—Request the patient to kneel on a chair then touch the floor. Since the knees are in a bent position, patients with true back pain or sciatica should be capable of performing the test with little difficulty, while those with non-organic back pain are generally unable to do so.

OTHER USEFUL SIGNS INDICATIVE OF
NON-ORGANIC PAIN (63)

- If the patient limps into the examination room, check the shoes for uneven wear if occurring over long duration. Canes, neck braces, and lumbar supports evidencing no sign of wear are indications of behavioral problems.
- If manual laborers claim inability to work for protracted periods, examine hands for calluses, periungual dirt, and lacerations. Muscle mass will rapidly dissipate during periods of inactivity. Thus, maintenance of upper-body muscle tone can be considered improbable in inactive patients.
- The observation of simple activities, such as removing a jacket or shirt, is demonstration of range of motion that involves the shoulders and neck, differing with testing range-of-motion measurements.

- "Everything hurts" upon light touch is an example of psychological aberration.
- The opposite of an antalgic gait. During gait analysis, it is noted that more time is spent on the defective leg than less.

Not considered a legal term, malingering is medical in basis and used within a social context, at times resulting in fraudulent behavior that is legally prosecutable. Malingering, which might cause an individual to be terminated from their job, is characterized by symptom exaggeration and feigning.

Clinical data, medical records and collateral information in particular, can often prove to be valuable resources in the assessment of malingering. In relation to disability claims, individuals will often exaggerate the severity of impairment, either consciously or unconsciously, particularly in those cases that might affect the outcome of receiving monthly benefits.

Assessment of the validity of a patient's complaints can be performed utilizing psychometric testing, in particular the MMPI-2 (Minnesota Multiphasic Inventory 2), the VIP (Validity Indicator Profile), and the P-3 (Patient Pain Profile). These tests can provide somewhat objective evidence in support of more subjective suspicion of malingering, and are administered by professional psychologists well-acquainted with this type of medical practice.

False imputation refers to the attribution of actual symptoms to a cause that bears no relationship to it. Two main situations for which a confirmation of malingering diagnosis can be ascertained include (1) an individual who is of the belief that they are unobserved and thus discovered to be engaged in activities they earlier asserted to be incapable of performing, and (2) the patient offers a stated confession of having feigned illness or injury. Accumulating all collateral data, including prior medical records, in combination with progress notes that provide substantial evidence for disproving a claim, is another option for ascertaining a diagnosis of malingering.

California initiated the first program to deal with Workers' Compensation fraud, reporting a decrease in claim payments totaling $2 billion per year for three consecutive years following 1993. The California-based Fireman's Fraud Insurance Company aggressively managed against fraud (26, 27, 28), saving a total of $10 for every $1 expended on defeating fraud, and included an investigative staff who possess professional backgrounds in the field of law enforcement and examine on average 1500 claims per year. Paul Conway of the Fireman's Fund states: "Most people won't commit a crime. People didn't know cheating insurance was a crime. You have benefits. If you're hurt, we'll take care of you. But if you claim to be hurt, and you're not, we're also going to take care of you, but with law enforcement." In acting as a deterrent and providing documentation necessary to prove fraudulent intent, Mr. Conway has also recommended that employees sign forms that state they understand Workers' Compensation fraud to be a crime.

PROFILE

An injured worker should be considered for claim investigation if a background or work history conforming to a malingerer's profile exists, with both employers and coworkers usually willing to reveal and substantiate these traits. Malingerers generally display neither interest nor pride in their work role, arriving late, exerting sufficiently little effort to meet satisfactory performance requirements, and frequently call in sick. They possess no loyalty to either employer or company (91), and are not traditionally averse to receiving pay for not having worked at all, even if payment totals less than normal earnings.

Any disgruntled employee facing potential termination might well be defined as a candidate for the filing of a fraudulent claim. Another possibility might include an event that is not witnessed by others, easing the process considerably in producing an uncontested account of the incident. Questions might be raised in such cases, including determining if the employee was in an area for which no authorization was obtained. In any case in which the disability claimed is disproportionate to the alleged injury, suspicion should surface to sufficiently warrant investigation of the incident.

FACTITIOUS DISORDER

Diagnostic Criteria for Factitious Disorder (81) include:

1. Patient might be accompanied by others to the evaluation or treatment sessions; however active collusion and victimization rarely occur.
2. Causation might be fabricated.
3. Detection of false symptom reporting.
4. Symptoms cleverly simulate genuine illness, appearing fascinating bizarre to cause sufficient concern to health professionals.
5. Frequency of whining and complaining, along with demonstrable hostility when confronted directly.
6. Poor treatment response in order to protract the role of ill patient.
7. Often associated with Borderline Personality Disorder, these patients frequently assign blame to others for their difficulties. In such cases, a relatively minor injury might well be considered responsible for the patient's current state of dysfunction, in addition to a host of other concomitant problems that, through careful investigation, prove to be an integral component of the patient's lifestyle and ongoing for extended periods over the course of their lifetime. In rare cases, the patient might not be injured at

all, but symptomatology is evidenced in the form of self-castigation, allowing the individual to obtain gratification as deriving from their need for emotional support, sympathy, pity, or other modes of caretaking possibly based upon early childhood deprivation and parental neglect.

8. Personality Pathology or strong characteristics in one or more the following:

   a. Borderline

   b. Passive-Aggressive

   c. Self-Defeating

Intention production of physical signs and symptoms in the absence of external incentives defines Factitious Disorder, with these individuals displaying false symptomatology or self-induced illness as means to receive attention and gain sympathetic support from others, monetary benefit not being the prime motivator in these individuals. As masterful artists of deception, the syndrome has been termed "Munchausen Syndrome," in tribute to the infamous German baron renowned for his ability to fabricate events in an extreme and flamboyant manner. Individuals presenting with Factitious Disorder are excessively desirous of medical attention as well.

Generally, treatment of this disorder includes counseling, rarely involving drug treatment therapies. Ironically, those patients who advance these pretenses to illness are, in fact, genuinely ill, yet rarely seek the care of the appropriate treatment physician, that of a psychiatrist.

Several characteristics (60) of the symptomatology of Factitious Disorder include:

- Inconstant symptoms, altering on a day-to-day basis.
- Changes in symptomatology not related to treatment but, rather, influenced by environmental factors.
- Unconventional and often symptoms bordering on fantasy and the fantastic.
- Association of a large quantity of symptoms that occur simultaneously or successively with one another in medically uncommon manner.
- Display of extensive medical knowledge.
- Tests often produce negative results, followed by further symptom development and progression.

It is hypothesized that minor variations of this disorder exist in which a worker experiences a minor injury, then prolongs the recovery period in order to perpetuate the sick role as means to achieve attention and sympathy. An individual with the major disorder does not work, and thus would be unlikely to seek treatment in an occupational medical clinic setting for an acute injury.

SOMATOFORM DISORDERS

Somatoform Disorder (77), characterized generally by inexplicable physical symptoms, is discussed in this section in relation to its variability in degree, with the disorder taking on less intense characteristics and for which an occupational medical clinic can be utilized for treatment purposes.

It is theorized that somatizing patients express and convert psychological and emotional distress into physiological-based symptoms, with complaints and symptomatology not considered to be volitionally-controlled. It has often been observed in individuals with difficulty in outward display of emotion; a valid manifestation of such might be that "the body will cry when the eyes cannot." A valid assessment of the somatizing patient requires considerable expenditure of time and highly honed skills to ascertain the full range of symptoms, concerns, and operant belief systems of the individual, with definite avoidance of excessive testing recommended. Patients need reassurance that their presenting symptoms and distress are being weighed heavily and taken seriously prior to assisting them in the ability to "reframe" their condition in a different light.

Patients with Somatization Disorder often engage in lower levels of physical activity than is considered normal, remaining bed-ridden on the order of from two to seven days per month, and possessing higher rates of disability and impairment to social activity, including difficulties in marriage and parenting. Individuals falling into this category are also observed to overutilize health care services, often incurring nine times the average costs in health care expenditures compared to normal individuals.

No definitive therapeutic treatment presently exists (6, 67) for Somatization Disorder, considered a chronic condition with poor prognosis. A potentially effective treatment for these patients is that of cognitive behavioral therapy. The term, cognitive behavioral therapy, refers to treatment that includes a number of component procedures. Some of these components may be called "behavioral" such as relaxation, social skills training and management. Others are described as "cognitive" because they address factors such as expectations, perceptions, and interpretations (82).

What somatic *amplifiers, cues, and drivers* exist in this patient?

A good example of a somatic cue might be described as follows: A roomful of people in which one individual coughs, then it is noticed that others follow suit by coughing as well. Thus, the first individual's cough acts as a cue or initiator for others to cough, and is considered within the normal range of human behavior.

Somatic amplifiers, on the other hand, include the perception that the cough is an indicator of sign of illness, with patients in this category having the tendency to amplify what is traditionally considered a benign phenomenon to that imbued with pathological meaning.

Somatic drivers can be distinguished by two types, those complaints originating from a misinterpretation of normally-occurring physiological sensations and amplified to a level of illness, and those individuals who possess a higher and more intense degree of reaction to normally-occurring environmental stimuli.

Understanding individual response levels to various cues serves the medical practitioner well in learning effective intervention approaches in order to dispel these perceptions and symptom drivers, enhancing the patient's ability to reframe his or her interpretation of these sensations. One method in which to dissipate these perceptions that cause intensified symptomatology and response might include requesting the patient to maintain a journal or diary that records pain increases, the activity he or she was engaged in at the time of pain event, as well as their thoughts and mood or emotional base (12). The information gained from such a journal can then be analyzed in conjunction with the medical practitioner during the next visit, serving to measurably assist in determining what pain drivers are active for each patient and formulating a plausible evaluation and treatment solution. Frequently, it is difficult to alter the deeply-ingrained perceptions and behaviors of these patients. Change requires an exertion of effort, with the easier and more manageable course being to maintain the status quo, despite change proving beneficial. Treatment requires considerable time and patience on the part of both the patient and medical practitioner.

Patients view their symptoms as perturbations or annoyances to be overcome, rather than limitations to their lifestyles. The primary goal for these patients is that of improved functioning to the greatest extent possible, with an increase in physical activity generally associated with a heightened sense of well-being, thus a reduction in symptomatology.

In general, the majority of individuals feel healthy most often, becoming ill only on occasion. In direct contrast, somatizing patients feel ill preponderantly, only occasionally experiencing a sense of good health. This distorted image is in dire need of reversal best accomplished through restoring a sense of control over symptoms and learning the co-relationship and interaction between stress and symptomatology.

According to the most recent worker-related surveys, conducted by NIOSH (National Institute for Occupational Safety and Health), greater than 29 percent of the American workforce currently describes their jobs to be "extremely stressful" on a daily basis, with individual workloads for many employees having exponentially increased. In today's culture, the stock market remains open on a 24-hour basis, email arrives continuously and relentlessly, cell phones help maintain constant contact with business environments, even while individuals are off-duty and physically inaccessible, and many employees thus perceive themselves to be workplace victims rather than freely-motivated individuals, enjoying their respective contributions to society daily.

For those patients who experience pain, stress reduction will in most cases also decrease symptomatology. Thus, stress management techniques should be made a component element of treatment for such individuals.

COMPENSATION NEUROSIS

The diagnostic criteria for Compensation Neurosis (81) include:

1. Frequent false attribution, in which the patient in fact has the actual disorder and symptoms, but then sets out to methodically and intentionally plan and devise a means in which to transfer real symptoms to that of an alleged cause.
2. Maximization of current medical and psychological problems, often in melodramatic ways. Highly dependent patients might also emphasize past problems.
3. Excessive exaggeration or prolongation of genuine injury following the time in which trauma has healed. In particularly entrenched cases, the symptoms actually worsen over time, and underlying the voluntarily displayed façade, the actual symptoms have either attained remission or attained a low-level and stable state. In order that medical and other observers better understand the gravity of the condition, the patient often overstates or dramatizes symptom intensity, consistently maintaining a high complaint level.
4. Patients often display excessive dependency and a clinging nature, remaining in treatment for lengthy duration.
5. Often considered the most common Disorder of Simulation in its dependency-inducing ability, frequently perceived as an extremely alluring facet generally accompanied by a real-life injury or illness, and one for which the patient is enabled to extend, exaggerate, or amplify in its true proportions.
6. Pathological personality characteristics, with strong elements in one or more of the following:
   a. Antisocial behavior
   b. Narcissistic
   c. Borderline personality

d. Passive-Aggressive behavior
e. Obsessive-Compulsive behavior
f. Dependent personality
g. Self-defeating behavior

STRATEGY

The traditional methods of treatment protocols for those patients obstinately maintaining the sick role often prove unsuccessful. These individuals desire the clinician to focus on symptomatology as means to camouflage the patient's own problems with compliance, drug-seeking behaviors, and overutilization of medical services. Therefore, the clinician must engage in a strategy of symptom management, patient psychological game-playing, and the medical provider's own sense of being victimized and manipulated. The focus should remain more focused on containment, less on curative factors and resist the temptation to attack or enmesh oneself in the circle of symptomatology. This is in contradistinction to the conventional or disease-oriented method of practice where the sickness is from physical pathology, or patient-centered clinical method (207) which, in addition to disease, focuses on the patient's illness experiences. The disease-oriented method is doomed to failure because of a lack of physical pathology. The patient-centered method will run into trouble in trying to find common ground requiring physician and patient to reach agreement on the nature of the problem, the goals of treatment, and the roles of the doctor and patient.

The solution lies not in withholding service or care, but in assessing the likelihood of a serious disorder or condition, weighing carefully both the risks and benefits of each procedure. In fact, a simple focus on compliance can prove itself far more valuable than a $1 million work-up of an otherwise perplexing symptom.

The cornerstone of effective management is predicated upon the organization and formulation of a trusting doctor-patient relationship, often established over time. The Healthcare Professional should assume the responsibility to develop and nurture rapport with the patient through empathetic behavior and signals, establishing in the process meaningful dialogue through appropriate and effective communication techniques. Other crucial elements of information might include testing performance results, treatment response, life and medical history, review and evaluation of medical records, and statements attributable to other informants. Oftentimes, the occupational medical professional operates without benefit of long-term follow-up treatment and meetings with the problematic patient who possesses underlying and preexisting psychological disorders and difficulties. Thus, these individuals are optimally managed outside the Workers' Compensation system.

Manipulative patients will often be observed to exploit those physicians on tight schedules through the use of implication that certain medications will solve their problems, referrals to specialists frequently requested, or that yet another diagnostic test might identify the "real" problem. These shortsighted solutions frequently result in often-critical delays rather than enhancing or contributing to long-term resolution of a particular individual's problems.

In some cases, composing a *Problem List* might be valuable in discerning actual rather than patient-offered causes for problems. Such a list might include prior medical history with multiple sets of providers, numerous attempted treatments that failed, history of rootlessness, and lack of social support systems, all of which might demonstrate compliance as the primary obstacle to health, not symptomatology or patient complaints.

Management strategies might include the creation of a *path for the resolution of a specific problem*, with clearly demarcated parameters along this pathway that indicate progress in developing cooperation in the patient toward advancing the restorative process. Low-level assignments such as maintenance of a diary or journal can serve to effectively alter the patient's perceptions but, more importantly, compliance will work to confirm the patient's intention as will the inclusion of family members in the therapeutic process, who can greatly enhance patient understanding and satisfactory compliance levels.

Clinicians often experience difficulty in distinguishing between factitious disorders and noncompliant, intractable, and treatment-resistant patient behavior. Chronic patients are often apt to create such high degree of discouragement as to compel some clinicians to dismiss them from treatment. The critical element in management of these patients resides in formulating a history of truth-telling, unlike the untruthful individual who is known to consistently distort, convolute, manufacture, or withhold relevant information and are not merely noncompliant in behavior, but suffer from simulation disorder.

The confrontation of clinical deception is a task not eagerly assumed by the majority of clinicians. Confrontation is often accompanied by conflict and subsequent hostility, with patients threatening vindictive retaliation and the filing of complaints at times. These patients often transfer to alternative medical providers as well, securing legal support to persist in their efforts at pretense and charade. The best method and approach to cases such as these that emerge in the Workers' Compensation system is to deem these patient's problems as non-work-related, stating your reasons clearly for such assessment, and discharging the patient, thus allowing the legal and judicial system to evaluate the case. You have performed and met the criteria of your job to the best of your ability under often-insufferable circumstances.

SUMMARY

Clinical management strategies related to the difficult patient involve the following steps:

1. Analysis and interaction with the patient to formulate an accurate diagnosis through the establishment of rapport using empathetic techniques and maintenance of effective communication mechanisms.
2. Reassessment of initial evaluation, then reevaluation through a process of assessing patient progress on a weekly basis. Reviewing the past can frequently offer a more enlightening perspective than judgments made currently. No fear should attach to revising the initial diagnosis and/or treatment regimen.
3. Proffer a professional opinion seeking consultation when and if deemed necessary.
4. Maintain effective and reliable communication techniques and cooperation with all parties involved.
5. It is customary to sense something is wrong upon first encounter with the delayed recovery patient. In order that these individuals do not "fall through the cracks," it might enhance the process to place their name on a board to keep track of weekly progress. The natural tendency is to suppress these patients from memory considering their ability to provoke discomfort and adverse feelings or reactions, a temptation to be resisted if and when at all possible.
6. Determine whether satisfactory treatment compliance has been achieved. Converse with the physical therapist in regard to his or her opinion and assessment of the patient.
7. Contact employer regarding whether conflicts have arisen in the past or presently exist with patient supervisor, and attempt to attain potential solutions for these frictional situations.
8. Once the underlying problem has been determined, whether psychosocial, malingering, or others in its basis, it is now imperative that a potential solution be developed to include alternative treatment method, applicable in cases in which a problem is construed as being non-medical in nature. The employer and insurer both possess expectations that we, as medical practitioners, perform in this capacity as well.

9. Keep patient informed of your opinion and, if in disagreement with your assessment, he or she can is free to request another professional evaluative opinion. Maintain a professional attitude at all times, avoiding any tendency toward shouting matches or verbal discordance.
10. It is important that the physician possess the ability to rapidly acknowledge and recognize problem cases, and formulate a determination as to patient motivation and desire.
11. Be equipped to recognize the difference between organically and non-organically-based disability factors.
12. Of equal importance to treatment strategies is the ability to recognize when to cease treatment, as no substitute for clear and sound judgment exists.
13. In all cases, medical care should be directed toward the injured worker assuming responsibility for his or her own health and rehabilitation.
14. The physical therapist should serve in the capacity of educator in order that treatment continues, with the hoped-for outcome that of full incorporation into work-related and everyday activities for the injured worker.
15. Treatment goals for patients with chronic pain should include drug detoxification, reduction in cure-seeking activities, and pain control mechanisms, gradually increasing activity levels and, finally, full-range return to work-related status.
16. Critical to the entire management process is the achievement of an educated and informed injured worker. Optimally, each patient should be well-informed of his or her medical diagnosis, expected course and treatment duration, and medical prognosis. This information assists the patient in gaining a greater sense of control of the disrupting elements of the condition, aids in avoidance of the sick role, and gauges or measures the return-to-work plan.
17. Patients presenting with somatoform tendencies often sense a strong compulsion for validation of their pain. The physician thus has the opportunity to assume the role of educator, explaining that the symptoms derive from a disorder of the autonomic nervous system, with future efforts directed toward the identification and reduction of those psychological stressors that serve to worsen the patient's degree and level of pain and discomfort.

Although the preceding discussion focused primarily on the disadvantages inherent in this type of work, advantages certainly exist as well, one of which includes the practitioner not having to interact with difficult patients on a long-term basis. Non-work-related problems necessitate referral to the patient's primary medical care provider. Work-related illness and injury are treated until permanent and stabilized status is achieved, with patients subsequently being released from treatment on a permanent basis.

The near-term future of occupational medicine need not concentrate its focus on merely the elimination of physical employment hazards, but in the long-term and permanent reduction in workplace stress and stressors to the greatest extent possible while simultaneously instructing workers in more effective coping mechanisms. We can safely and with some predictive accuracy hypothesize that these methodologies will produce the most beneficial and positive influences in reducing injurious activity in the workplace environment, thus maintaining employee well-being and productivity (13, 121). In order to best serve and formulate treatment regimens for employee-related illness and injury, in particular in a technologically transformed and continually advancing techno-centric society, the occupational medical practitioner will greatly enhance treatment modalities and recovery processes by consideration of these newly-emergent stressors and stress-related activities that now adjoin themselves to America's workplace in the twenty-first century.

Chapter Ten

The Corporate Medical Director

> . . . .*and I have not thought it beneath me to step in workshops of the meaner sort now and again and study the obscure operations of the mechanical arts.*

> —Bernardo Ramazzini, 1700

FUNCTIONS

All corporate medical departments are widely divergent, each with its own history and culture, confronting contingencies that vary substantially from one to another. Corporate medical departments serve three primary functions, as follows:

1. *Medical*—Functional Core of Occupational Medicine
   a. The individual health assessment
      i. Fitness for duty
      ii. Matching workers to jobs.
      iii. Assessing work-relatedness of disease
2. *Environmental*—Medical Surveillance
   a. Monitoring is conducted directly through inspection of the workplace and indirectly through biological testing and clinical evaluation of probable or suspected employee exposure.
3. *Organizational*—Policy and Planning Activities
   a. Guidelines for implementation of newly formulated and revised corporate health policies and procedures.
   b. Auditing of Occupational Medicine program.

c. Training and professional development and continuing education for
staff health professionals.

ROLES

Corporate medical directors serve in two essential capacities: *employer*-
oriented managers, and *employee*-oriented medical physicians (156), the majority of which possess distinctly varied medical backgrounds and education.

Clinicians generally hale from private practice, the professional nature of
which is defined by patient care. Society's expectations include the requirement that a physician assumes the role of clinician and, as such, his or her reputation is predicated upon this underlying premise. Little, if anything, instills
and maintains the confidence and support of both employees and management more than the prompt and expert treatment of work-related critical illness and/or injury (140).

Scientists generally emanate from backgrounds spanning preventive medicine, toxicology, and/or occupational health fields, their philosophical
grounding and educational training based in population groups or scientific
theory and hypotheses of a broad scale rather than individual health care.

As means to develop and evolve more important objectives, direct involvement in the daily operations of clinical services is the pragmatic approach utilized by most corporate medical directors. The ability to perform
medical care for patients on a one-at-a-time basis affords the medical director the ability to glimpse, for all practical purpose, the patient population at-
large, the focus of which should be his primary objective.

EFFECTIVENESS

Up until the 1950s, the large majority of knowledge regarding disease was
obtained through study of clinical material and resources, collected from the
archives of physician private practice. Epidemiology and statistical analysis
transformed these methods to that of evidence-based medicine, vastly improving medical practice.

In order to perform at optimum effectivity, the corporate physician should
have the capability to effect and influence change in areas such as job design
and environmental engineering, as well as the psychosocial aspects of the
workplace setting. And, in order to accomplish this, the corporate physician
should ideally assume an integral role within management infrastructure,
working from within to successfully develop and achieve necessary transi-

tions in the medical environment, the cost of which can often be prohibitive. One major challenge confronting the field of occupational medicine has historically included the avoidance of conflicts arising between management and labor while simultaneously offering beneficial contributions strongly valued by both. This can, of course, create tricky maneuvering and finessing on the part of a conscientious and effectivity-driven medical director.

A zone exists for which the company or corporate structure is clearly held accountable for job-related effects on employee health, as does a sphere in which the employer cannot be held responsible in those cases for which job-related activity is deemed to not affect or impact worker health issues. The middle or central area existing between these zones is one of wide ambiguity, in which cause-and-effect relationships between health and labor-related issues are poorly understood and accountability requires adjudication on a case-by-case basis. Despite management and labor possessing fundamentally and often polar opposite interests, the medical organization can only function at maximal levels if cooperation and harmony are objectively pursued (141).

For the good of the composite organization, that which comprises both management and employee and not least of which places patient care as its primary function, corporate medical directors should be both averse to and resist conflict of interest situations, such as becoming party to job actions by distinguishing between their roles as doctors and personnel officers or, for example, in cases in which an employee claims illness yet the company voices disagreement with this assertion. The latter issue generally involves entitlement policy, such as sick pay, disability insurance, absence with pay, and compensation benefits. These issues are not favored by unions when decided by medical directors due to their potential to create bias toward the company structure.

By giving precedence to the individual needs of employees, occupational physicians best serve their organizations owing to the aggregate positive impact and benefits a given occupational medical program will provide to its employees individually. When the focus is clearly placed on the physical and emotional health of each employee, the results will be higher levels of productivity and general harmony within the corporate infrastructure.

MANAGEMENT

As described by Frederic Winslow Taylor (42), "scientific management" is a way to resolve employer/employee conflict, requiring acceptance of the premise that a single, unanimous scientific solution to a given problem can be attained, independent of either social or political context. By virtue of the authority based in technical expertise accorded the corporate physician, he or she plays an active role in this aspect of management. From this we formulate the question of how can members of the scientific community exert influence over those who assume power positions. The higher one moves up the hierarchical scale, the less probability exists that problems are solvable through preprogrammed algorithm; the more complex the structure, the deeper the need for expertise and, needless to state, all experts lend substantive contributory value to the prestige and self-esteem of their employers.

The individual armed with the more profound levels of knowledge are thus both more vigilant of and within the range of achieving more opportunities and any and all concomitant potentially resulting consequences therefrom. The executive equipped with an understanding of problems that might ensue from data and knowledge, who grasps both the limitations and contributions of educated and well-versed professional individuals, is indeed also the more likely to temper and negotiate power with wisdom (145). Pragmatically, the cohesion of knowledge and executive privilege and management, along with the mollification of potentially conflict-inducing or threatening circumstance within the corporate medical infrastructure can serve as a beacon of guidance and direction in what otherwise might result in irresolute and potentially perilous friction. An approach based in assuaging the two camps, if you will, working to harmonize and filter out otherwise detrimental elements will serve to benefit the whole and its component parts equally well.

COMPETING INTERESTS

It is customary in medical practices for both the physician and patient in combination to jointly pursue and achieve the primary goal of restoration and maintenance of employee health without benefit of external sources. However, should the physician be under the employ of a medical organization, the objectives and goals of that enterprise might not only differ from but encroach upon the predominant focus, which encompasses the patient's specific needs; nonetheless, this intervening variable should not influence major judgments concerning the welfare of the patient (147, 148, 149). Radical departure from this basic tenet can often be encountered in cases in which the medical practice that serves at the behest of a specific organization has as its principal function issues non-medical in nature, for example, within corporate occupational medicine environments, military medicine, and sports medicine settings. Those engaged in practices such as these are often working within environmental pressures derived from their organizations, stressors that must be carefully weighed in relationship to and against the professional interests these individuals represent. The basic mission of bureaucratic medical delivery systems is to administer patient care, whereas in contrast, the mission and objective of corporate medical practices is that of profit-bearing returns on investment. Despite the traditional thinking that professional and bureaucratic forms of control are, in basis, an incompatible twosome (150), the reality counters that proposition in the common threads and compatibility evidenced in these two ostensibly divergent fields of medical delivery (151, 152).

The expertise of corporate medical directors melds well with the technical core of organizations (153) in which a product results. Thus, an employer is seen to exert control over both the physician and patient alike through the activities of the medical practitioner, a situation that enhances the complexity of both the patient and physician roles, subjecting occupational medical practitioners to conflicting and competing expectations. The nature of this intricate structure can work to divide and disrupt loyalties of corporate physicians, ascribing to them coercive authority over their patients and, in so doing, inserting a line of discordance between the medical practitioner and his or her patient.

The question is then raised as to what level of autonomy does the corporate physician possess and, further, what degree of influence is the medical practitioner authorized to exercise within the organization itself? The predominating question arising from this is to categorize who exactly defines the client and what parameters comprise the problems for which the professional has been employed to solve? In large measure, corporate physicians do retain primary control within the technical domain (154), however, they are also identified as consulting professionals, expected to formulate problem resolution within the context of the organizational objectives and goals as set forth by management.

THE SCOPE OF OCCUPATIONAL MEDICINE (146)

—A synopsis of the consensus opinion from the *American College of Occupational and Environmental Medicine*:

> Corporate medicine and its practice have undergone significant change over the course of recent decades, promoted largely by shifting expectations and perspectives evidenced in society. The specific content of each program is largely dependent upon organizational functions, activities, and the potential hazards present in the workplace. The primary concern of corporate medical programs of necessity must include the protection of worker health, in addition to any other human populations potentially placed at risk of exposure to environmental injury or illness. Programs catering to medical delivery in the workplace should resist any attempt to serve exclusively at the discretion and interest of

management, labor, attorneys, and/or government, focusing instead upon its objective goals of worker health and satisfaction.

ESSENTIAL COMPONENTS

- Employee Health Evaluation
  - ° Pre-placement evaluation
  - ° Periodic medical surveillance evaluation
  - ° Post-illness or injury evaluation
- Diagnosis and Treatment of Occupational Injuries and/or Illnesses
- Emergency Treatment of Non-Occupational Injuries and/or Illnesses
- Program Implementation for Use of Personal Protective Equipment
- Evaluation, Inspection, and Abatement of Workplace Hazards
- Toxicological Assessments
- Maintenance of Occupational Medical Records
- Immunization Programs as Prophylactic Measures for Occupational Infections
- Periodic Evaluation of the Occupational and Environmental Health Program
- Disaster Preparedness Planning focused on Workplace and Community-based populations
- Rehabilitative Assistance for Employees Identified with Substance Abuse or Emotional Problems
- Palliative Treatment of Disorders to Enable Completion of Employee Work-Shifts
- Repetitive Treatment of Prescribed and Monitored Non-Occupational Conditions and Concurred with by Personal Physician (Physiotherapy, injections)
- Assistance to Control Illness-Related Job Absence
- Assistance in Evaluation of Personal Health Care
- Immunization Program against Non-Occupational Infectious Diseases
- Termination and Retirement Evaluations
- Participation in the Planning, Provisions, and Assessments of Quality of Employee Health Care Benefits
- Participation in Systematic Research Projects
- Administration and Organization

PREVENTIVE MEDICINE

As a preeminent component of prevention programs, the screening of healthy individuals for early detection, identification, and treatment of disease plays a significantly critical role in preventive medicine. Long viewed as the primary mission of Occupational Medicine, preventative medical interventions are the logical thread leading to substantial and sensible ends for a medical specialty dealing with human populations engaged in workplace activity and are deemed to be relatively healthy. Lifestyle-oriented health-risk appraisals as well as risk-reduction programs administered at worksites have increasingly gained wide acceptance, with preventive medical programs initiated via the screening of healthy populations as means to search out subgroups within the larger populous who are at elevated risk for preventable illness and/or disease. As example, obesity and smoking greatly increase the considerable probability of experiencing coronary artery disease and cancer, yet surprisingly some percentage of individuals possessing these risk factors will suffer no ill-effects despite these ill-advised behaviors and predilections. The incapacity to forecast or predict which of these individuals will be fortunate, preventive measures are all-inclusive in their application, with the preponderance of current energy focused on and dedicated to discovering creative and innovative means by which to encourage individuals to engage in activities that will expand their lives and benefit their lifestyles despite their preferences to not do so.

ENVIRONMENTAL MEDICINE

Clinical environmental medicine is the study of detectable human disease from exposure to physical, chemical, and biological factors in the environment (208). Recent research has uncovered evidence linking environmental exposures to common adverse health outcomes. For example, there is an association between air pollutants and increased mortality from cardiovascular diseases (209), asthma (218), and cancer (217). Studies have demonstrated a relationship between lead exposure and impaired intelligence (210,211), and exposure to cadmium with decreased bone mineral density (212). The Surgeon General's report, Healthy People 2010 (213), outlines a set of goals at lowering the risk of environmental related disease to air quality, water quality, toxic pollutants, and toxic waste contaminants. Within the public health arena, the disease process involves what is termed a susceptible *host* with an infectious or toxic *agent* in a conducing *environment*, the causative chain of which can be severed by altering any one of these three variables. Within the framework of safety and health-oriented programs, focus is trained on the host for individual-based programs, the agent and environment for environmentally-oriented programs, along with circumstances that coalesce in combination with the host.

DISABILITY MANAGEMENT

On average, 3.9 percent of the American workforce is absent from the workplace as a result of unscheduled reports of illness, according to Wyatt, in a report entitled *Staying at Work: Integrated Disability Management around the World: 2000/2001*. Employee absence incurs costs averaging 10 to 15 percent of total payroll expenditures, estimated at 150 percent of an employee's wage plus wage replacement costs. Thus, for an employee earning $20.00 per hour, this cost incursion could total as much as $45.00 per hour in terms of absence (157). Only a fraction of the total costs of absence, direct benefit costs are based on lost revenue calculations, with productivity loss, as based on this measurement, incurring as much as three times the direct benefit costs of group health and total disability program expenditures combined.

Should a business enterprise choose to not install a program for reduction of absenteeism, such as that of disability management, rates of absence are apt to increase to levels as high as 5.3 percent. In contrast, the company that elects to implement such programs witness absentee rates frequently as low as 1.4 percent (158).

According to Dick Lewis, Senior Partner with LewisCo, a disability consulting and case management firm in Deerfield, Illinois, a 30 to 40 percent increase has been evidenced in long-term disability, with some insurance companies experiencing rates as high as 5 cases per 1000 employees with coverage, increasing from 3 per 1000 ten years ago. The aging population of baby boomers is, in all probability, a major contributor to this rate increase, with a proportionate rise in disability incidence to the aging of a population.

Unlike the past, in which all employee benefit programs, such as health, sick leave, short- and long-term disability, and Workers' Compensation, were compartmentalized, Integrated Disability Management refers to the cohesion and coordination between these respective departments working in conjunction along with the business enterprise, the common goal of which is to resolve a given employee conflict or problem and return him or her to full-spectrum work-related activity as rapidly as possible (159). The success of programs such as these are predicated on the premise that the majority of employees willfully desire a return to work status, with only a small percentage content to draw upon disability compensation, despite being capable of work-related activity. Offered the opportunity, the vast majority prefers to expend their energies and time in work-related activity in contrast to the tedium of visiting one doctor or another, subjecting themselves to a myriad of testing procedures and, in frequent cases, battling the system. As pointed out by Steve Schrenzel, Managing Director of The Governance Group of Summit, New Jersey, most of the population can be found to define themselves through their jobs and related work activities, as distinct from marital status, educational background, hobbies and/or leisure-time pursuits. A large majority defines themselves and their philosophical proclivities via the professions and work-related responsibilities they engage in on a day-to-day basis, often finding the notion of retirement and/or disability to be anathema to their need to thrive and attain success.

Returning to work prior to a *disabled mindset* entrenches itself in an individual can have major implications for one's sense of self-worth and esteem. Disability, as a mind-body process, refers to the functional impact an injury or illness wages on the patient, varying considerably from one individual to another. Whereas some individuals possess high tolerance levels for pain, functioning at near-normal levels despite the discomfort, others exhibit a low-level tolerance for functioning under high degrees of stress or pain, their functioning ability markedly deteriorating on a plane that objective measures would otherwise suggest. Dramatic factors that affect this observable variability in patient response to disability include prior education and learning experiences as well as current social context.

An effectual evaluation of disability cases (160) can be critically assisted through the use of the following two approaches:

- Treatment of the patient as an individual; and,
- The utilization of the principles of population management to develop optimum intervention techniques.

The accomplishment of these two objectives can be greatly enhanced by categorizing disability populations into three distinctive types, as follows:

1. Patients presenting with well-defined acute or progressive illness or injury, the prime intervention of which is that of physical health care.
2. Patients presenting with well-defined acute or progressive illness or injury for which behavioral health factors play a prominent role. Health outcomes and return-to-work timelines are jointly determined by physical and emotional/behavioral health factors.
3. Patients presenting with emotional/behavioral health problems for which the primary intervention is that of mental health therapies or chemical dependency treatment. Response to behavioral health services is the primary determinant for return-to-work timelines and work capacity.

Experience has proven that, while the patients comprising group one account for a significant proportion of work-related disability, the vast majority of poor health outcomes and return-to-work successful results are prevalent throughout groups two and three.

Ironically, the system provides individuals a vested benefit and interest in maintenance of disability. In the course of struggling to obtain benefits, these patients fight assiduously for the legitimacy of their disability claims, finding it extremely difficult to relinquish. Formerly healthy individuals, when confronted with disability, are often consumed with anxiety and fear when encountering the massive disruptions to their otherwise normal lifestyles, inevitably requiring them to determine how to proceed from this new vantage point. Disability and its associated physical and social issues continues to be plagued by poorly understood issues, involving not only physical illness and injury, but markedly influenced by personality, workplace stressors, the dynamics of interpersonal relationships, interfamilial, and financial-based factors. Further, a goodly amount of work absence is often rooted in stress-related disorders or socially-induced factors that interfere in extreme ways with physical rehabilitation and normal functioning capacity following injury or disease. The complexity of disability and its concomitant issues that inhere from social, psychological, and economic factors, only add considerably to its perplexing nature and thus requires an interdisciplinary approach to its effective management.

Effective Disability Management (160, 161) mandates that both doctors and case managers alike pay careful attention to an individual patient's psychosocial environment, which can more readily be accomplished through the use of the following strategies:

1. Observe thoroughly the health care expert, mindful that primary care practitioners assume key roles in disability management, with optimum results occurring through frequent interaction of not only the doctor and patient, but doctor and employer as well. Generally, the majority of attitudes and belief systems of physicians support return-to-work and disability management functions, with the greater percentage of practitioners receiving basic needed information relating to job requirements acquired through patient communication.

2. Focus should be firmly placed on function, not cure, with the objective of effective management fully centered on functioning restoration of the patient rather than elimination of symptomatology. The significant element here is the return of the patient to work-related status, despite the possible discomfort of residual symptoms remaining, most particularly in cases in which symptoms do not interfere with patient capacity to perform work-related tasks. The facilitation and institution of modified-duty return-to-work programs are imperative if an effective management strategy is to be achieved.

3. Compassionate health care delivery with a firm posture is essential to the requirements of effective disability management, requiring a mixture of

empathic understanding and determination. Crucial to this strategy is the ability to be flexible in cases in which one approach has not proven to be effective, or in situations in which newly-acquired facts suggest the utilization of a different course of action.

4. Clarity in defining what constitutes disability, the majority of employers blueprinting specifically-defined parameters of disability and usually is applicable to loss of capacity to perform the intrinsic tasks of a given job.

5. Prioritize return-to-work status as the objective goal. A large majority of programs offer return-to-work instructional classes that provide practical coping skills and additionally address the potential psychological barriers encountered by employees following long absences from work-related activity.

6. Formulate the criteria for functional return-to-work status. The benchmark and centerpiece for return-to-work status should include functional capacity, not the elimination of distressing physiological or mental and/or emotional symptomatology.

7. Counteract secondary enforces. Secondary gains are often applicable to situations in which medical and/or behavioral problems persist, in part due to social and/or financial reinforcement. A prototypical case might be that of the patient who is eligible for full-salary status over a 90-day period of short-term disability, however this patient instead views this as a three-month vacation. With no avoidable means by which to curtail or deter the impact of secondary reinforcement, by providing the employee an aggressively clear return-to-work message, in combination with shortened disability timeframes, one can effectively forestall some of the negative impacts of secondary gains.

8. Develop and establish reasonable work-related plans using a phase-in process in which the worker returns to job-related tasks based upon time or environmental accommodation for specified periods. Enabling more flexibly constructed procedures for return-to-work schedules will greatly enhance the employee's desire to successfully achieve full-spectrum return-to-work status.

9. Utilize economic pay-based incentives to increase the value of return-to-work status, providing a safety net that ensures it is perceived as a worthwhile endeavor, not a hardship to be endured.

Disability Management requires a marriage between patient, physician, and employer, working in concert to formulate a participatory partnership, not an adversarial relationship.

Early initiation of contact with human resource departments, case managers, and direct supervisors will set the tone for all that follows. Direct and sincere communication is elemental and critical to effective management, in contrast to ambiguous and mixed messages, which often serve to exacerbate symptoms. The more one can foster and maintain open lines of communication between the three participating members of this partnership, the higher the probability exists that the employee will desire a full-status return-to-work capacity.

Be mindful when dealing with claims managers, the most carefully designed plans often derailed when encountering a confrontational and abrasive individual charged with the responsibility of managing claims.

The intricacies and complexity of disability issues involve emotional and behavioral drawbacks as well as the physiological strain on both employees and their families. Corporate culture and business enterprises thus require the compassionate and understanding hand of managers who possess the capacity to clearly delineate and give voice to the needs of claimants, providing assurances that their requirements are equitably and fairly-judged. Effective disability management strategies, of necessity, must therefore knit together a cohesive format for which the participating members, that of employer, employee, and physician, can ably accomplish the objective goal of restoration and rehabilitation of the disabled employee, the absence of which will impact negatively on medical outcomes, further discouraging return-to-work status. If harmony and non-adversarial interconnections are established between these three parties, all the more likelihood positive restorative disabled employee outcomes will be achieved. In understanding that physiological injury and/or illness is but a single element in the disability arena, it is incumbent upon the corporate medical director to assume fully cognizant knowledge of the emotional and behavioral-based issues that accompany disability status. Through a continuum of communication between the employer, employee, and medical practitioner we can continue to formulate, develop, and institute innovative and creative measures for beneficial change throughout the Workers' Compensation system based in harmonizing influences rather than adversarial conflict.

Chapter Eleven

Potential Solutions

PAST HISTORY

Workers' Compensation laws have been witness to many changes since their inception, in large part resulting in temporary solutions to what has since become a more permanent dilemma. Improvements to situational or momentary problems without paying much heed to the larger landscape and, as time proceeded, other, at times more intractable difficulties emerged causing the passage of further legislation. This piecemeal approach to an intransigent and complex system results from and is the product of bureaucratic and political systems in their attempts to satisfy individual constituencies with self-serving interests. Employers look toward government to solve steadily increasing costs to the Workers' Compensation program and its consequent impact on the overall health of business enterprise in the United States, while employees rely upon government to likewise address inherent inequities in the system and obstacles that would otherwise safeguard the health and welfare of workers and work-related environments.

Traditionally, government assumes the role of mediator between the employer and worker populations, one side generally feeling either intimidated or victimized by the other side, thus becoming more vociferous and gaining political strength in the process. In most cases, this behavior acts as significant impetus to promote legislation favoring, in most cases, the more vocal of the groups and, as time progresses, the opposing side with less political clout experiences the ill-effects of the oppressed as the recent legislation takes effect. In a kind of seesaw effect, this oppressed group now presses for yet further legislation to remediate its perceived inequities, acting much like a pendulum as it swings in phases from one group to another, first bestowing favors on one, then another political action group contingent upon the vocal acuity of each.

Presently, the Workers' Compensation system is prototypical of the psychological adage "the squeaky wheel gets the grease," promulgating and promoting the behavior we witness between the parties involved, yet neither side desiring the appearance of having been too satisfied, lest it result in a loss of some benefit or other further on down the road. The question then arises as to why government assumes the role of benevolent grandparent, in effect, treating both workers and employers alike as though spoiled children, providing temporal comfort to their frustrations in the form of minuscule, incremental gains that, unfortunately, result in satiation on a temporary basis.

A meeting convened in 1972 by the National Commission on State Workers' Compensation Laws would now serve us well to be reconvened in order to conduct an independent study of the current problems plaguing the system, subsequently formulating recommendations for changes to the presently-existing laws, free from the tentacles of political and bureaucratic entities. Notwithstanding this pending occurrence, the following solutions to these complex and often perplexing problems are offered and discussed in brief below.

RECOMMENDATIONS

Recommendations for improvements to the presently existing Workers' Compensation system are as follows:

1. Those providers administering medical treatment to injured workers should be capable of passing certification requirements by a reputable licensing agency in order to ensure both competency to perform the responsibilities inhering to the occupational medical field as well as provide uniformity across all State Workers' Compensation systems.
2. Alter the disability award system as it currently operates? A recent survey by the National Council on Survey Insurance says that 60% of all benefit costs are from permanent partial disability (134), with over 40% of awards in California being less than 15% (214). These individuals are not seriously injured and are working at their regular job so why should they be compensated in a no fault system?
3. Formulate and facilitate an employee counseling service in order to better serve those employees experiencing worker-related injury and/or illness in order.
4. Employee supervisors should be mandated to undergo periodic training programs in conflict resolution in order to both recognize and mediate between adversarial parties within the workplace environment.

CERTIFIED MEDICAL PROVIDERS

A wide body of research has been both conducted and with it an expansive degree of knowledge is available in the field of occupational-related injury. When appropriately administered and applied to the care of patients, it cannot be refuted that this vast resource material can and will produce beneficially positive treatment modalities and outcomes. For example, the management of back pain, the most common of human afflictions following that of the common cold, has been researched and numerous studies conducted the world over for many decades and, as a consequence, protocols have been developed and established in the treatment of acute back-related injury and pain. And, understandably, these regimens are traditionally and regularly adhered to due to their ability to generate high degrees of recovery over the short-term while incurring lower expense rates, more positive outcomes, and decreased probability of developing treatment side-effects. Therefore, should medical providers elect not to follow these aforementioned protocols, certification should not be granted to treat these patients, as these practitioners are no doubt doing a disservice to both the patients and field of occupational medicine alike.

As laws presently exist, medical providers are authorized to treat injured workers, including those for whom their practices are limited in scope and in which no available means by which to perform appropriate assessment of the "total patient" exists, a proven necessity in treatment of these patients. Rather, these providers should be employed as consultants as opposed to assuming the role of primary treating physicians. As described in the earlier section dealing with management of difficult patients, problems occur when the medical history of a patient presents in a cryptic or misleading manner as distinct from the actual illness. A prime example might be the patient who presents with neck or shoulder pain or discomfort which, in fact, might be unrelated to an affliction of that anatomical site, deriving instead from a physiological difficulty in another body location. Those medical providers possessing limited scope of practice, for example chiropractors and acupuncturists, might be more apt to treat only those anatomical areas as described by the patients, unfortunately remaining oblivious to any underlying pathophysiological processes related to somatoform disorders.

A well-formulated, clearly elucidated certification process as executed by an organization would substantially provide for and ensure both the quality of care and competency level of those medical providers administering to injury-related workers. This process would benefit not only the primary parties involved, that of the worker, employer, and insurance company, providing assurances of not being victimized or exploited by the system, but barriers of

mistrust will be eliminated as well, enabling all parties to be more cooperative while promoting a less adversarial environment.

TRANSFORM THE DISABILITY AWARD SYSTEM

The disability award system has posed a legal conundrum for the Workers' Compensation program, with the 1908 observations of Franz Kafka, not long after the
inception of the first Workers' Compensation system as established in Germany
by Bismarck over 100 years ago. In order to establish a method for determining
what categorized disability in human terms, German physicians decided upon a
system based upon the number of symptoms the patient presented with, thus the
higher the quantity of symptoms, the deeper the level of disability. Kafka (1883-
1924), employed as an insurance adjuster in Germany between the period 1908
and 1921, had as his primary duty the responsibility of traveling to industrial accident sites in order to formulate an assessment of worker injury, and ultimately
leveling a determination as to what compensation should be received by these
individuals. In the process, Kafka became well-acquainted with both the victims
of the system and the opportunistic seekers of retribution, the result of which
produced his literary works reflecting his inner sense of the anxiety plaguing human existence, experiencing pervasive alienation in an unintelligible, hostile,
and indifferent universe. It has often been suggested that this negative belief system resulted from his dealings with the extreme frustration of his professional
employ within the German compensation system.

The underlying methodology from which the disability award system is
based has been fundamentally flawed since its inception, in radical need of a
complete transformation. For example, medical examiners use joint range-of-
motion as the basis for measurement of disability, known to demonstrate poor
correlation with actual degree of disability. Despite this knowledge, medical
disability examiners continue to carefully perform these measurements to determine a percentage of permanent disability despite little scientific basis.
Within the framework of a no-fault system (the present workers' compensation system), why should a disability award be provided to a worker capable
of performing his or her previous job? The argument in favor of compensation is based on a theory that, perhaps someday, this worker will have to com-
pete in the general marketplace and a residual impairment diminishes his or
hers attractiveness for a job compared to other applicants. Since the advent of
the ADA (Americans with Disability Act of 1990) legislation this concept appears to be outdated and irrelevant to the true reality of the situation.

Widely perceived to be overcompensated, partial permanent disability awards
are often ostensibly the main source of abuse evidenced in the present Workers'

Compensation system. If payments of this nature were to be eliminated, the often prolonged, low-yielding success of the medical treatments and high-cost legal fees likewise would disappear as well, resulting in savings of from 25 to 50 percent in Workers' Compensation expenditures. A permanent partial disability award is not a settlement because the case remains open after the determination of the award (based on a theoretical residual disability). This award is in addition to medical payments, temporary total disability payments, and rehabilitation payments. Injuries for which permanent partial disability claims are made range from paper cuts to amputations and from paralysis to sprains. In each case, unless the parties can reach agreement on the amount to be compensated, the claim of the employee is heard at a full hearing with an arbitrator (judge) at the workers' compensation appeals board (court). The decision of the judge can be appealed higher up in the court system by either party. The attitude of the judges, even in seemingly minor cases or well healed injuries, is in part based on considerations of sympathy and politics and in part based on reality. There is a belief that, in many instances, seemingly minor injuries have long term consequences that do not appear until far in the future, like 20 years from now and the injury may make the employee susceptible to other infirmities, like arthritis, to a greater extent than the general public. So the system, many times, becomes adjudicated based on medical and social intangibles (215). Furthermore, there are certain non-medical factors which are considered important and serve to adjust the award to the upper or lower ranges. Adjustment for age has been argued both ways; higher for the younger person because of having to live with the disability for a longer time or higher for the older person in getting accepted for employment with an accompanying impairment, because of age discrimination.

Another factor, which should be irrelevant, but of great importance is the amount of lost time by the injured employee. In Illinois, a two week lost time back strain is worth significantly less than a sixteen week lost time back strain even if all the findings after two years are identical in the two cases. The relationship between the injury and the type of work which the employee performs is another variable; the effect of a back injury on a sales clerk will not be evaluated as severely as a back injury to a heavy laborer. Other factors of subjectivity coupled with the forgoing discussion would account for the extreme variability in this unfair award process and substantiates the argument for its elimination.

EMPLOYEE COUNSELING

In cases in which a worker and supervisor are engaged in disagreement or conflict, the result might be the worker filing a Workers' Compensation injury or work-induced stress claim. With average costs of claims in California approximating $45,000 as of 2003, this activity appears markedly disproportionate as compensation for an individual who deems oneself to be offended or slighted. Currently, there exists no alternative avenue to best resolve conflicts of this nature. In cases in which union involvement exists, the worker is more apt to file a grievance with a union steward, thus initiating a hearing in which resolution of the conflict might ensue. However, the worker might still be inclined to file a Workers' Compensation claim, dependent on his or her perceived concept of the injury. One potential solution to this situation might be to facilitate mandatory conflict resolution counseling between the parties to include a 30-day waiting period prior to the filing of a stress claim, in effect allowing a cooling-off period which might well have the effect of reducing stress-induced claims by 50 percent.

SUPERVISOR TRAINING

As the intermediary between management and labor, the employee supervisor is often considered to be the key source of conflict in the work environment—the "man or woman in the middle" as it were. This individual is often deemed to have the worst job in any business enterprise—scrutinized, surveyed, and dogged by upper management, mistrusted by subordinates, and responsible for satisfying production quotas by inspiring and generating high levels of employee productivity. Each employee responds in unique ways to different incentives, thus the inevitability exists that a certain percentage will be offended. The unions are well-equipped to recognize that supervisor conflicts often form the foundation of the majority of worker-related grievance. Therefore, it is not unreasonable to surmise that measurable investment in training programs catering to supervisory interpersonal relationships will produce a considerable net return vastly larger in magnitude than the initial investment through marked reductions in Workers' Compensation claims.

Focusing on the interchange between supervisory-level individuals and employees or subordinates in today's business environment will prove highly satisfactory in the future, both short- and long-term. Those who are employed in lower-level jobs require supervisors that are not simply in place to force the hand of management, but to compassionately and firmly understand the work environment, of which the employee is an integral part. Communication skills without question play a significant role in establishing a harmonious environment for workers and serve to dramatically reduce stress, most especially in high-pressure and deadline-oriented settings. The ability to communicate well with employees will not only enhance the productivity levels of a business enterprise, but will likewise reciprocally work to lessen the weight and burden the supervisor experiences as well in attempting to achieve and satisfy the increasing demands of management. When workers are given the opportunity to confront a supervisor with grievances, and receive in return an empathic ear along with the perception to understand the underlying difficulty experienced by an employee, harmonizing influences will prevail.

Supervisor training programs oriented to enhancing communicative skills and proficiencies will thus provide long-range security for business enterprises equipped with the ability to manage and resolve potentially destructive and cost-prohibitive claims that otherwise might produce protracted and antagonistic legal recriminations.

SUMMARY

If one were to accrue only one benefit or gain in knowledge from the field of Occupational Medicine it would be to *Keep an Open Mind*, to adhere to flexibility in both attitude and application as essential elements in the art of problem-solving. Dealing with and managing human behavioral problems can often be extremely complex and daunting in their intricacy, with those of us as practitioners experiencing and witnessing multiple instances of deceptively misleading medical histories offered by patients. These seeming manipulations and creatively-designed camouflages can often be viewed to be both bizarre in nature and often highly suspect, and more often than not concluded to be cases of simulated injury disorder. However, that can also be misconstrued and subsequent events will often evolve in such a way as to disprove this determination, as the patient is disclosed to be a completely work-oriented, honest, and well-meaning individual, for whom treatment is successful and is rapidly dismissed from the system through prompt recovery.

In yet other cases, patients often begin the treatment process presenting as both cooperative and genuine in their discomfort, yet as time progresses it is proven that these appearances are both deceptive and manipulative (78). Without hesitation, those in the field of Occupational Medicine have been party to those individuals who might well take advantage of a situation wholly contingent upon whether or not an opportunity exists for deception. In other words, a major influencing factor in such a scenario is based upon the medical practitioner's degree of ability in detecting and managing deceptive behavior, as well as his or her knowledge and awareness of such cases. Multivariate factors apply when dealing with the two systems of human nature and the Workers' Compensation program. Largely dependent on demographics and corporate culture locales, *difficult patients* in any given practice will

vary most probably between that of five and fifteen percent of the total patient base. Those who desire to manipulate and exploit the Workers' Compensation system will do so facilely when one considers that few safeguards
or preventative measures exist to deter such behavior.

In order that no injured worker be declined appropriate treatment, that all
are treatment with equitability in quality and level of care, the Workers' Compensation system provides no obstacle to obtaining medical treatment. The
single requirement embedded in this system is that the worker report his or
her injury to the employer, from which point the process is mobilized. As
well, the system easily facilitates an employee victimizing the system if anger
or antipathy exists, targeted at the employer or supervisor, and repudiation or
vindication is sought. There exist as well those instances in which poor work
performance is determined to be the cause of an employee's pending termination and, if this individual is simultaneously in the process of being under
the care and treatment for a work-related injury and engaged in modified-duty
work status, it becomes all the more difficult for the employee to be terminated. This type of employee is generally not terribly inspired to work but,
nevertheless, is interested in receiving compensatory benefit in the form of
money in order that he or she is no longer required to work; or, an individual
in this position might simply be possessed of an underlying and undetectable
hidden agenda, not easily visible to employer or management.

Human exploitation of vulnerabilities and weaknesses inherent in society
is historically well-known and considered a de facto method of conducting
day-to-day business in many cases; society allows for a given percentage of
any known quantity in societal establishments and systems for this type of behavior, as built-in costs and losses. Whether applicable to an attorney taking
advantage and license with a legal loophole, or an individual using the
proverbial "sick day" to be absent from work, these behaviors fall inarguably
under the heading of unethical activity; manipulation in and of itself cannot
be construed to be illegal—we have all encountered on a daily basis those
who are manipulative by nature. The aberrant behavior of one who engages
in outright falsehood in order to benefit monetarily, however, can very well
be deemed fraudulent behavior, thus legally prosecutable if the facts substantiate the allegation.

Formulating judgments regarding patient behavior is generally frowned
upon and considered an impropriety for health care professionals to engage
in. As medical providers and experts, our educational training dictates equitable treatment for all patients, irrespective of the cultural, social, and economic background of any patient, a standard that in all likelihood originates
long in the past, when priests assumed the roles of physicians by medically
ministering to patients. By virtue of the work itself, occupational medicine

has redefined this disinterested and non-prejudicial status for medical practitioners. In order to guarantee and insure the rights of other primary stakeholders in the system, it is a necessity that the medical practitioner is equipped to some degree with the ability to ascertain the verity of a worker's behavior in terms of work-related injury. This ability is integral to the administration of medical care in an effective and sound manner while simultaneously protecting the rights of the primary stakeholders in the Workers' Compensation system; not an easy task by any measure.

Employers are precluded from either gaining access to or delving into a given employee's health status, as promulgated by the Medical Privacy Act. Rather, this type of information must be obtained through means of a health professional, limited to furnishing only that information which directly pertains to worker health and safety.

At times, an employer or insurance company will consciously create barriers to appropriate management of patients, as covered in Chapter 3 of this book under the section "Other Stakeholders." The current system of managed care in the United States has encouraged a climate and environment in which the perception of the patient is that he or she must demand services, envisioning the medical care establishment with suspicion and skepticism, a negative mien that has unfortunately begun to flow into and permeate the Workers' Compensation system arena as well, with some percentage of patients hoping to utilize this system for their ailments. Better stated, managed care providers have, in some cases, communicated to their patients the notion that their injury or illness is work-related when, in fact, it is not, as means by which to avoid treatment under a given managed care insurance policy. These kinds of behaviors only further complicate and entangle an already difficult to manage and navigate system, adding yet another rationale for a major revamping and transformation.

Secondary to any given trauma or disease are numerous and intricate psychosocial factors (78), all of which necessitate further acknowledgment and evaluation as adjuncts to the treatment of the physiological disorder as means to ensure successful therapeutic outcomes. Each *symptom* is comprised of *two* quite distinctive segments, as outlined below:

- The *physiological component*, the foundation of which is based on the pathophysiology of medical science. Based upon the manner in which the injury or disease physically interacts with an individual, this component can be termed the *logical* part of the symptom.
- The *emotional* component, known also as the *individual psychic signature*, is reflective of the internal idiosyncratic meaning or context in which the individual perceives or attaches to the disease, pain, and discomfort. In

terms of the scientific rubric of medicine, the basis of its teachings and min-
istration, this component bears no logical context for which the medical
practitioner can relate; the emotional fabric of a given patient derives and
is a reflection of his or her early life experiences, lying dormant at times until such time as a physical event of extreme measure or degree allows it to
emerge and thus provide opportunity for its expression (74, 88).

The need for individualized medical treatment is informed primarily by the
unique nature of the *individual psychic signature*, a measurably greater element to be considered than the physiological variations in response to any
given illness by a particular patient. A fund of medical guidelines and procedures exist, yet few standards or guideposts for a particular disorder that allow for the distinctive and quite disparate social and cultural backgrounds of
individuals; as humans we share commonality in physical characteristics, yet
it is rare to encounter those same similarities in emotional makeup and design. In essence, we are human beings in the body of animals. In order to experience a sense of complete medical care administered by competent and
compassionate professionals, we all desire to be acknowledged and appreciated by those for whom we have emplaced trust on the highest plane, the safe-
guarding of our lives and healthful well-being.

There appears to be little appreciation or understanding of how occupational medicine impacts societal and community health, both physical and
emotional. By assuming a direct and active role in the professional playing
field of injury and illness prevention programs, concomitantly ensuring a
healthful societal environment, the medical practitioner provides higher standards of quality of life and professional settings that travel far beyond the
scope of the mere treatment of industrial-related injuries. Human-related activity and interaction are highly contingent upon self-realization and actual-
ization, often if not always affiliated with an individual's sense of achievement and accomplishment and most certainly attaching to professional and
career-related activity. Despite the human discourse and dream of retirement
from the world of work, setting one free from the burdens and stresses of
work-oriented landscapes, perhaps the highest level of accomplishment is often derived from one's work. One would be hard-pressed to refute the concept that the greatest rewards and sense of fulfillment emanate from the challenges and competitiveness of either satisfying or exceeding the normal
expectations in labor, whether it be within the framework of professional or
sub-professional work status. Seldom can one encounter the opportunities afforded individuals to soar and progress as humans external to the workplace
environment. The field of Occupational Medicine resides in the rarefied atmosphere and holds the uniquely distinctive position of being the only med-

ical specialty oriented exclusively to maintenance of that environment, the workplace infrastructure and the ever-growing populous that inhabits that dwelling. As practitioners, we therefore both prescribe medical treatment and receive the benefits innate to such an esteemed and singularly important role, and should therefore measure its success based on the efforts we ourselves exert in formulating innovative, creative, and visionary means by which to accelerate its improvement and ultimate effectivity. This book has attempted to advance the progress of just such efforts by all of us that count ourselves amongst the fortunate to be engaged in such rewarding and purposeful labors. If we, both as individuals and collectively, maintain positive attitudes and remain flexible in our engagement with the public, our patients, we can certainly not only improve upon the present system of Workers' Compensation, but vastly transform its basic structure to one for which we can all be proud, and likewise enhance the health and well-being of the patient population for which we have been entrusted.

Chapter Twelve

Case Histories

There is a limit to wisdom,
But there is no limit to foolishness.

—An old saying in Turkmenistan

CASE #1. THE DOG BITTEN PATIENT
THAT BECAME PARALYZED

Source: The author's files.

L.B., a 42 year-old Visiting Nurse, provides services at her patient's home, driving her own car for transportation. After entering a client's home, she realized she left her bag in the car. After retrieving it, she turned outward in exiting the car, and was assaulted by a stray Pit Bull dog that attacked her. She suffered injuries to her forearms and hands, and the dog ran away and was never found, no one having witnessed the events. The dog seemed to emerge from nowhere and disappeared in a like manner.

When she was brought to the office, she was hysterical, crying, and very sensitive to pain. Actually, her injuries were not severe. Multiple superficial skin abrasions and scratches were noted primarily on both outer aspects of her forearms and on the dorsum of the left hand. They were not the typical wounds usually inflicted by a dog, because of the lack of lacerations, or deep penetrating wounds. The wounds were cleaned and dressed and subsequently healed without infection.

Since the search for the dog was unsuccessful, she was started on the rabies vaccination series. Seven days after the first injection she developed a sudden onset of complete paralysis of the right upper extremity accompanied by lack of feeling to pinprick testing. The extremity demonstrated flaccidity, but no fascic-ulations or change in the reflexes were noted. The Babinski tests were negative. MRI scans were performed on the cervical spine and brain and were normal, and a neurology consultant thought the disorder was non-organic. At the time of fol-low-up visits in the clinic for dressing changes, she displayed no apparent frus-tration with the paralysis and seemed to accept it as a matter of course. [At the time, I thought to myself, if this happened to me I would be very upset if I couldn't move my right arm or hand.] She smoked with the other hand, and had her husband accompany her and help her with her needs. She even seemed calmer than she was previously. She displayed what has been described as "La-belle Indifference," observed in conversion hysteria.

She completed her rabies vaccination series with no other neurological se-quelae. Concern over the differential diagnosis of the paralysis as possibly caused by a reaction to the vaccine was mitigated by recommendations of the manufacturer and the patient's wishes to continue the series.

When observed two months later, she appeared to have made a complete recovery when she was in a dance club performing vigorous movements with her extremities with no apparent residual.

This disorder meets the criteria for conversion hysteria, but the entire his-tory displayed histrionics, requiring much attention by the healthcare providers, and she was unable to work during the time period. Factitious Dis-order and Malingering were also possibilities, but academic unless the patient volunteers more information. Her care was transferred to an internist.

CASE # 2. THE DISHONEST LABORER
WITH A CHANGING HISTORY

Source: The author's files.

J. M., a 34 year-old laborer, presented to the clinic complaining of pain in the right shoulder and right elbow. He stated that he helped lift a wall frame with other coworkers, 5 days before, and as he pushed it up into place, he felt a pull in the right shoulder. This was on Thursday. He worked the next day with pain in right elbow and right shoulder. He reported the injury on Mon-day and presents to the clinic for evaluation.

Evaluation revealed marked tenderness on palpation of the right elbow joint with pain on extension, and marked tenderness over the right acromio-clavicular joint. X-rays revealed a non-displaced fracture of the radial head and a partial acromioclavicular separation.

The disorder did not coincide pathophysiologically with the mechanism of injury. This had to occur from a recent fall rather than from lifting and pushing.

He then claimed he fell of f the roof of a house five months before, at work, but didn't report it. This revelation also is inconsistent with the findings. My determination was that his injuries were not work-related and he was referred to his private medical doctor. Finished? Not quite.

He obtained an attorney who referred him to an orthopedist two months later for another opinion, who stated he thought it was work-related. The orthopedist did not have my report for review. Instead, he obtained the history directly from the patient, who told him he reported the injury right away and I sent him back to work, forcing him to go to his own doctor. He had been on disability for five months and still not recovered at the time a deposition was taken by an attorney representing the Insurance Company. No surgery was performed. He was being treated with back manipulation and physical therapy without improvement in his symptoms.

My opinion of this case is that it represented false imputation. The disorder was probably caused on the weekend, while off-duty, and reported it as a work injury Monday morning.

The worker used the legal system to challenge one opinion against the other, to collect disability benefits while off work, and eventually hopes to obtain a settlement. However, a deposition revealed he was terminated for cashing a paycheck belonging to a fellow employee shortly after I saw him. Furthermore, the fact that the attorney's consultant failed to review my report probably invalidates his report. These facts are encouraging, but another Independent Medical Examiner will have to reexamine the issues in this case and make a determination. His case will eventually need to be adjudicated by a Workers' Compensation referee in order to determine the validity of his claim.

CASE # 3. THE WAREHOUSE WORKER WITH A HERNIA

Source: The author's files.

A 28 year-old male presents to the clinic complaining of a painful bulge present for the past few months in the left inguinal region. As a cotton warehouse worker who was hired nine months ago without a pre-placement physical, his job requires heavy lifting at times. The work being seasonal in nature, he filed the claim after being laid off. The employer called and requested the healthcare provider determine if this was work-related.

Examination revealed a left inguinal hernia requiring surgical repair. The patient was questioned about both his prior work history and examinations. He stated that he had a pre-placement evaluation about 15 months ago at another medical clinic when applying for another job.

Medical records from the other clinic documented a left inguinal hernia present on the examination they performed 15 months ago, which was prior to coming to work for the present employer. My conclusion, therefore, was that the hernia was preexisting and not work-related.

This case demonstrates the value of obtaining prior medical records when assessing the veracity of a worker's history. The information can prove invaluable in resolving disputes. The employer was fortunate to have had this readily available information, or otherwise he would have had to bear the burden of responsibility for the claim. He was trying to save money by not doing pre-placement physical examinations.

CASE #4. A BACK INJURY WITH NO PRE-PLACEMENT PHYSICAL

Source: The author's files.

J. R., a 36 year-old warehouse worker, came to the clinic complaining of severe low back pain after heavy lifting at work. He failed to improve with conservative care, subsequently undergoing an MRI of the lumbosacral spine. The report stated that there was a herniated disk at the lumbosacral junction that was essentially unchanged from a previous study on file two years earlier.

Further questioning revealed the following:

- He had a prior work injury two years ago, resulting in a permanent partial disability award of 40 percent.
- He was restricted in his lifting capacity to 50 lbs.
- He was off work for two years until hired in this new job two months ago, requiring lifting of 100 lbs. on occasion.
- He received no pre-placement physical evaluation.
- When questioned as to why he took this job with these physical requirements, his response indicated that he thought he was rehabilitated because his back pain had subsided prior to starting work again.

Patient confidentiality laws prevent the employer from inquiring into an applicant's prior medical history. Thus, it is so important for applicants to be evaluated for fitness for duty through a pre-placement evaluation conducted by a healthcare professional well-versed in Occupational Medicine. The Workers' Compensation law states: "The employer takes the worker as he finds him," and thus is responsible for treating and rehabilitation despite any prior injuries or disorders. The difficult problem for this case is that since this individual was precluded from lifting more than 50 lbs on a prior partial permanent disability award how can he return to a job requiring lifting 100 lbs.? He can't; therefore this employer will have to absorb the cost for job retraining.

CASE #5. THE HOTEL WORKER CLAIMING JOB STRESS

Source: The author's files.

J. S. is a 26 year-old Hotel Worker who presented to the clinic complaining of severe anxiety and depression symptoms of recent onset. He claimed this to be from work stress and harassment because of his homosexual orientation. He has worked at the hotel as a food server for one year and experienced no problems until the past few months. Some of the other male employees made gestures like blowing kisses, facial gestures, and effeminate movements because of his gay orientation.

Upon clinical examination, it was revealed that he displayed anxiety, tremulousness, and hyperactivity. He also experienced insomnia and was unable to continue at work. His presentation possessed all of the attributes of a work stress situation, save for the fact that many of the other employees were gay as well. I inquired with the work manager as to the status of the other homosexuals at the workplace, and it was revealed that there were no other complaints. There existed a work culture that was "gay oriented." Thus, why should this individual be singled out? An in-depth past medical history revealed the following:

- He was diagnosed with bipolar disorder during his late teenage years.
- He was on Social Security Permanent Total Disability for four years prior to securing his present job.
- He was well-controlled on medication, until he gradually ceased taking it over the course of the preceding 6 months.
- He was placed back on medication and began displaying improvement.

Considering all the facts, it was obvious that he was suffering from a previous uncontrolled psychiatric disorder, masquerading as work stress. Although the playful actions of the other employees contributed to his distress, the major source of his problem was that of Bipolar Disorder, and thus not work-related in this State.

CASE #6. THE PAROLEE ON A WORK PROGRAM

Source: The author's files.

A 38 year-old parolee participating in a work program was given early release from prison on condition that he resides at a halfway house and work at a car wash. During the first week of his job of drying off cars, he fell in an area that he was restricted from (the Lube section), and fell on his left side. Those who witnessed the event claimed that it appeared to be purposeful.

Clinical evaluation revealed primarily low back pain, but no objective findings were present. He could bend and touch the floor. He was placed on modified duty; he however refused this option due to the severity of symptoms. Observation by the other parolees at the halfway house detected no impairment of his movements. It appeared he was malingering. He was returned to full-duty and discharged from treatment.

He refused to return to duty. Because he was not working on the work furlough program, he was returned to prison. He obtained an attorney who secured his release from prison and referred him to the attorney's customary orthopedist, used traditionally for his evaluations.

The orthopedist conducted a medical examination, concluding that his injury was Bona Fide and that he indeed was disabled after all. His conclusions proved no positive physical finding, with the exception of a positive result on 3 out of 5 of Waddell's signs.

This case will be adjudicated by the Workers' Compensation Appeals Board. The reason for its inclusion in these case studies is as demonstration that each individual, even if within the jurisdiction of the prison population, is accorded the same rights under the Workers' Compensation system! Additionally, a well-developed industry exists to assist these individuals toward accomplishing their goals.

CASE #7. THE BRAIN DAMAGED PATIENT ACCUSED OF FRAUD

Source: *Los Angeles Times* (17) (August 6, 2000).

George Solis was a manager of a family restaurant. At the age of 56, while carrying a container of Jalapeno peppers, he was run over in a hit-and-run accident as he was crossing the street, sustaining brain damage as a result. His claim was that he was unable to perform his work-related duties due to this accident, and subsequently awarded $126 per week in Workers' Compensation benefits.

The Freemont Insurance Company, however, was considering the potential for awarding a substantially larger settlement for permanent disability several years later and, in doing so, conducted its own investigation to determine the extent of Solis' brain dysfunction. In the process, Freemont secured the services of a private detective, who in turn videotaped Solis in his normal everyday activities. The videotape included footage of Solis engaging in flag football, race-walking, and driving a vehicle, despite him having stated to an insurance company physician that he was unable to conduct his normal activities independently without the assistance of others, nor did he possess the ability to drive a vehicle any longer. After viewing the videotape, this same physician concluded that, based upon the activities Solis engaged in, evidentiary proof of malingering by Solis was quite apparent.

Based upon the declarations of the physician, the District Attorney issued a warrant for Solis' arrest, and agents were deployed to his residence in Huntington Park, bringing him into custody during the early morning hours. Upon her son's arrest, his 80 year-old mother screamed: "You can't take my son; my son is no thief!"

Deputy District Attorney Eleanor Daniels conceded that Solis' initial injury was valid, and in so stating to the Los Angeles Municipal Judge, Elva Soper, she claimed that his arrest was, rather, predicated upon behaviors of exaggeration, declaring, "the impairment is not as extensive as 100% disabled." Daniels' proclamation inspired Judge Soper to instead use her own powers of observation, and assumed a non-traditional stance during the initial stages of the case proceeding to appoint an expert of whose specialty included that of determining the mental impact of brain injury. Employed for the defense and using public funds, this specialist then conducted an examination of Solis.

The specialist, Dr. Robert Brook, viewed the secretly recorded videotapes, concluding that they provided irrefutable proof that Solis was, indeed, critically disabled. Brook predicated his evaluation based upon the observation that a time period of three minutes had elapsed for Solis to perform the task of tying his shoelaces, which, under normal conditions and for the average adult, traditionally requires only a time of less than one minute to accomplish. In an additional videotape demonstrating Solis engaging in the game of flag football, Brook surmised that, although Solis was indeed playing this game, he appeared from the videotape to be playing by himself, with neither his teammates nor the opposing team acknowledging his presence much less involving him in their game.

In viewing another videotape of Solis participating in a race-walk, the physician assessed that he demonstrated an inability to navigate much less excel at what is considered to be a traditional and fundamental stride used for this type of sport, causing Solis to thus be disqualified from participating in the race.

Dr. Brook concluded from his assessments that the only type of work-related activity Solis could ably engage in would include that of "simple, concrete, repetitive activities under constant supervision."

Based upon Dr. Brook's determinations, and over and above the objections of the District Attorney, the case was summarily dismissed by Judge Soper.

CASE #8. HEAD TRAUMA PATIENT ACCUSED OF FRAUD

Source: *Los Angeles Times* (17) (August 6, 2000).

A Guatemalan father of four, 35 year-old Edgar Huaz, was employed on the graveyard shift at a food plant in Vernon performing activities as a chicken deboner. Mr. Huaz leveled a claim that, during his work shift activities, an industrial-sized soap dispenser fell on his head in the Men's Room while he was cleaning up. He subsequently went to a hospital presenting with complaints of headaches and, within one month's time, in order to relieve pressure on the brain sustained by a bruise, known as a subdural hematoma, to that area, a neurosurgeon, Dr. Harley Deere, performed a surgical operation on Mr. Huaz.

The food plant employer secured the services of Freemont Insurance to refute Huaz's claim that his injury was work-related and, in so doing, evidence emerged that Huaz had participated in an offsite fistfight with a coworker shortly before undergoing brain surgery.

The inference assumed by Freemont Insurance indicated Huaz's injury as having derived from the fistfight, not that of the soap dispenser event incurred at his employment site. From this assessment, both the insurance company and Huaz's employer were of the belief that the claim should be denied, and found the District Attorney's office in ready agreement, subsequently charging Huaz with engaging in an act of insurance fraud.

Despite the above, the case lost its footing based upon the testimony of Dr. Deere, who ascertained that the fistfight was physically incapable of having resulted in the type of injury he discovered when Huaz's brain was opened during the performance of the surgical procedure. Thus, based upon Dr. Deere's statements, the District Attorney's office dismissed the case.

CASE #9. THE WORKER SUED THE INSURANCE COMPANY FOR MALICIOUS PROSECUTION

Source: *Los Angeles Times* (17) (August 6, 2000).

Employed as a data entry clerk for Blue Cross in 1991, Indravan Jayaswal initially visited a physician complaining that the neck, back, and shoulder pain he was experiencing was the result of work-related activity on computers. During an interview, Jayaswal stated that he elected to not file a claim at the time after being advised by a coworker that those who filed such claims often had their employment terminated.

Jayaswal was capable of managing his levels of pain until early 1995, during which time Blue Cross increased their productivity quotas, forcing

Jayaswal to also increase time spent at his computer. He then elected to visit a physician of his own choosing, who subsequently referred him to two specialists, to whom he described having experienced a sensation of pulling while he was engaging in lifting up his garage door. Jayaswal did not offer any mention of his pain as being related to work activity, despite being advised by one of the specialists that he would do better to refrain from work-related activity for a short time. Both the physician and Jayaswal then signed a State disability form, indicating by checking off a box that they were explicitly declaring that the ailment did not originate from work-related activity.

Based upon what the specialist had recommended, Jayaswal returned to his employment with certain limitations regarding computer-based activity. His supervisor then referred him to the Health and Safety Department of Blue Cross, where Jayaswal completed a Workers' Compensation claim form, declaring his pain to be work-related. The claims examiner, assigned to the case by Blue Cross' Workers' Compensation carrier, a Kemper company, was skeptical of the claim's merits after reviewing the statement signed by Jayaswal.

A physician, under the employ of an insurance company, voiced her own suspicions to the claims examiner as well, which resulted in Kemper then referring the case to the State Department of Insurance and the District Attorney's office for investigation and possible prosecution. Kemper officials asserted that they possessed knowledge that Jayaswal often filed false claims, although they later conceded this information to be unsubstantiated. They suggested as well that Jayaswal's claim filing was based in fraudulence as means to pay for medical treatment for which he possessed no group insurance, despite Jayaswal having used a group health plan to pay for his medical treatment.

A wholly inadequate and incomplete investigation was conducted by the Department of Insurance to determine whether Jayaswal's sustained injuries were work-related. And, once Jayaswal's case came to trial, testimony was given by one of his physicians stating that his injuries were in all probability very much related to his work-related activities. Despite this physician's testimony, the prosecution deemed this to be irrelevant, with Deputy District Attorney Robert Wallace putting forth the argument that fraudulence is contingent upon "state of mind," contending that it was not significant whether Jayaswal was eligible and entitled for compensatory benefits. Rather, if it could be proven that Jayaswal's attempt to secure benefits while under the belief that he was in fact not entitled to such compensation, that alone would be sufficient enough for a conviction.

Notwithstanding the prosecution's determination and subsequent case against Jayaswal, in disagreement with that assessment, Superior Court Judge Michael Tynan acquitted Jayaswal prior to any witnesses for the defense even being allowed to testify.

As one outcome to this case, Jayaswal filed a lawsuit against the insurance company based on malicious prosecution, ultimately reaching a settlement with Kemper for an amount undisclosed to the public. Despite success at winning a settlement, Jayaswal was unsuccessful in both attempting to regain his former state of employment with Blue Cross or even securing employment within the same industry. Reflective of his dismay at the events leading up to this unfortunate conclusion, Jayaswal, now 61 years of age, states, "They destroyed all my life. I was just interested in why I had pain. I had a good job. My company was paying a lot of overtime. . . . Why should I go to Workers' Compensation? I wasn't going to get much [money]. I only wanted the pain to go away."

Appendix

Attachment A

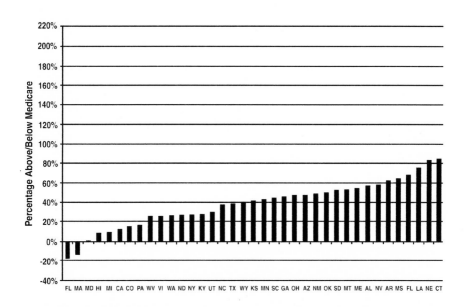

This diagram demonstrates the payments for workers compensation to medical providers compared to Medicare payment allowance in each individual state. Note the marked variations (97). Reproduced by permission from "Benchmarks for Designing Compensation Medical Fee Schedules: 2001-2002" by the Workers Compensation Research Institute.

Attachment B

A checklist for the healthcare provider that is a useful guide in determining malingering.

Barkemeyer-Callon-Jones Malingering Detection Scale(14)

II. Interview Behaviors
Instructions: For each of the behaviors described below, check those that occurred during your evaluation.
A. Introductory Phase: Spontaneous Comments by the Patient
_____ 1. The patient expressed exaggerated confidence in the examiner's ability.
_____ 2. The patient made statements or presentations that would appear to enhance his position in society.
_____ 3. The patient made denigrating statements about others in the immediate community.
B. History Taking Phase: Characteristics of the Patient's Presentation.
_____ 4. The patient focused on the severity of the reported problem.
_____ 5. The patient focused on the impairment resulting from the reported problem.
_____ 6. The patient's reasoning included no alternatives.
_____ 7. The patient made temporal associations that are not cause and effect relationships.
_____ 8. The patient described an atypical or very unlikely response to treatment.
_____ 9. The patient presented a constellation of symptoms that are not consistent with a pathophysiological abnormality.

_____ 10. The patient denied responsibility for clearly voluntary acts.

_____ 11. The patient's disability was emphasized during the examination to the exclusion of consideration of his abilities.

_____ 12. The patient denied the ability to learn new skills to compensate for those lost.

C. History Taking Phase: Manipulation Attempts

_____ 13. The patient cited another professional who allegedly agreed there was a problem.

_____ 14. The patient described the prestige of other people who allegedly found a pathological process.

_____ 15. The patient quoted an authority on the subject of the suspected pathological process.

_____ 16. The patient used an irrational analogy to justify a claim of physical pathology.

_____ 17. The patient threatened harm to himself or others if relief was not found.

_____ 18. The patient overstated the examiner's authority for intervening on the patient's behalf.

_____ 19. The patient implied there might be legal retaliation for a missed diagnosis or improper care.

D. Patient's Response to Questions.

_____ 20. The patient questioned the competence of the examiner.

_____ 21. The patient gave an affirmative response to an inappropriate leading question.

E. Examination Phase.

_____ 22. Any physical effort resulted in enhancement of the patient's presentation of symptoms.

_____ 23. The patient's responses during the examination did not support a physiological explanation.

F. Patient's Response to Disagreement.

_____ 24. The patient's response to the examiner's explanation suggested a distorted meaning of the examiner's statement.

_____ 25. The patient demanded an explanation based on inadequate data.

_____ 26. The patient questioned the examiner's motives.

II. Apparent Goals for Patient's Behavior.

Instructions: Rate each of the following according to the likelihood of their correctness. If the statement appears to be correct, place a check mark beside it.

_____ 27. The patient's complaints lead to the avoidance of a normal responsibility or a noxious activity.

_____ 28. The patient's complaints result in the gain of either a concrete entity or an abstract quality.

_____ 29. The patient's complaints result in the retention of either a concrete entity or an abstract quality.

Note: From Charles A. Barkemeyer, North Street Publishing Company, Baton Rouge, LA. Cutoff score of 7.6 on the 29 items revealed a hit rate of 95.1% (96.7% true positives and 90% true negatives). With permission.

References

1. Walker, E. A., Unutzer, U., & Katon, W. J. Understanding and caring for the distressed patient with multiple medically unexplained symptoms. *J. Am. Board Fam. Pract.* 11(5): 347–356, 1998.

2. Groves, J. E. Taking care of the hateful patient. N Engl. J. Med. 1978: 298; 883–7.

3. Hahn, S. R., Kroenke, Spitzer, R. L., Brody, D., Williams, J. B., & Linazer, M. et al. The difficult patient: Prevalence, psychopathology, and functional impairment. *J. Gen. Intern. Med.* 1996: 11: 1–8.

4. Russo, J., Katon, W., Sullivan, M., Clark, M., & Buchwald, D. Severity of somatization and its relationship to psychiatric disorders and personality. *Psychosomatics* 1994: 35: 546–56.

5. Eisenberg, L. Disease and illness. Distinctions between professional and popular ideas of sickness. *Cult. Med. Psychiatry* 1977: 1:9–23.

6. Speckens, A. E. et al. Cognitive behavioral therapy for medically unexplained physical symptoms: A randomized controlled trial. *BMJ* 1995: 311: 1328–32.

7. Smith, G. R. Jr. et al. Psychiatric consultation in somatization disorder. A randomized controlled study. *N. Engl. J. Med.* 1986: 314: 1407–13.

8. Yeung, A., Deguang, H. Somatoform disorders. *West. J. Med 2002*: 176(9): 253–256.

9. Calabrese, L. V. Approach to the patient with multiple physical complaints. *In*: Stern, T. A. et al. eds. *The Massachusetts General Hospital Guide to Psychiatry in Primary Care*. New York: McGraw-Hill: 1998: 89–98.

10. Haas L. J., Osman, S. N., & White, G. L. Jr. Caring for the frustrating patient. *Clinical Reviews* 11(10): 75–78, 2001.

11. Katon W., Von Korff, M. et al. Distressed high utilizers of medical care. *Gen. Hosp. Psychiatry*. 1990: 79: 89–99.

12. De Wit, R. et al. Evaluation of the use of a pain diary in chronic cancer pain patients at home. *Pain*. 1999: 79: 89–99.

13. Nugent, T. Take his job and. . . . *The Johns Hopkins Magazine*. Nov. 2002.

14. Barkemeyer, C. A. Malingering Detection Scale. Baton Rouge, LA: North Street Publishing.

15. McCoy, D. *Workers Compensation Claim Management Fraud Awareness*. <http://www.mccoyconsulting.com/fraud.html>.

16. HJH Group, Inc. *Trends in workers compensation.*< http://www.hjhgroup. com/fraud.html.>

17. Rohrlich, T., Larrubia, E. Public fraud unit favors those who privately fund it. *L.A. Times* (Sunday, August 6, 2000, Home Edition section): Part A, page A-1.

18. Katon, W., Von Korff, M., & Lin E. et al. Distressed high utilizers of medical care. DSM-III-R diagnosis and treatment needs. *Gen. Hosp. Psychiatry*. 1990: 12: 355–362.

19. Kroenke, K.M Mangelsdorff, A. D. Common symptoms in ambulatory care: Incidence, evaluation, therapy, and outcome. *Am. J. Med*. 1989: 86: 262–266.

20. Kroenke, K., Jackson, J. L., & Chamberlin, J. Depressive and anxiety disorders in patients presenting with physical complaints: Clinical predictors and outcome. *Am. J. Med*. 1997: 103: 339–347.

21. Kirmayer, L. J., Robbins, J. M., Dworkind, M., & Jaffe, M. J. Somatization and the recognition of depression and anxiety in primary care. *Am. J. Psychiatry*.1993: 150: 734–741.

22. Gureje, O., Simon, G. E., & Von Korff, M. A cross-national study of the course of persistent pain in primary care. *Pain*. 2001: 92: 195–200.

23. Kuch, K. Psychological factors and the development of chronic pain. *Clin. J. Pain*. 2001: 17: S33–S38.

24. Turk, D. C. Combining somatic and psychosocial treatment for chronic pain patients: Perhaps 1 + 1 does = 3. *Clin. J. Pain*. 2001: 17: 281–283.

25. The National Institute of Neurological Disorders and Stroke. *Chronic Pain*. 3 April 2001. <http://www.painconnection.org.>.

26. Jones, J. W. (1983). *The human factors inventory*. St. Paul, MN: The St. Paul Insurance Companies.

27. Jones, J. W. (1984). *The organizational management survey*. St. Paul, MN: The St. Paul Insurance Companies.

28. Jones, J. W., & Dubois, D. (1985). *The human factors surveys: Background and interpretation guide*. St. Paul, MN: The St. Paul Insurance Companies, 1–33.

29. Workers Compensation Research Institute. *The anatomy of workers' compensation medical costs and utilization: Trends and interstate comparisons, 1996–1999*. Cambridge, Massachusetts.

30. Atkinson, W. Is workers' compensation changing: *Living Wage*. July 2000: 45, No. 7.

31. United States Department of Labor. *Workplace injuries and illness in 2000*. USDL 01-472.

32. Fricker, M. Heavy caseload: More than 5,000 claims at SR appeals board. Press Democrat Online. <http://www.pressdemo.com/workerscomp /day3/appeals.html.>

33. *Workers Compensation*. July 2002. New York: Insurance Information Institute.

34. Freeman, V. G., Rathore, S. S., Winfurt, K. P., Schulman, K. A., & Sulmasy, D. P. Physician deception of third-party payers. *Archives Int. Med.*1999: 159: 2263–2270.

35. *Benchmarks for designing workers' compensation medical fee schedules: 2001–2002.* Cambridge, MA: Workers Compensation Research Institute.

36. *Executive survey of workplace safety.* Liberty Mutual Insurance Company, 2001.

37. Flor, H. Spouses' sympathy increases pain. *32nd Annual Meeting of the Society for Neuroscience.*

38. Ren, K., & Dubner, R. Central nervous system plasticity and persistent pain. *J. Orofac. Pain.* 1999: 13: 155–163.

39. Baker, Lawrence C., & Krueger, Alan B. Medical costs in workers' compensation insurance. *Journal of Health Economics*, 14 (1995): 531–549.

40. Centers for Medicaid and Medicare Services (CMS). Health Care Finance Administration website, *National Health Care Expenditures, 2000.* <http:// www.hcfa .gov/stats/nhe-oact/tables/tl.html>.

41. Ernst & Young LLP. *Treatment guidelines for low back injuries: A qualitative and quantitative analysis of the Industrial Medical Council and the Agency for Health Care Policy and Research Low Back Guidelines.* Prepared for the California Workers' Compensation Institute, June 1996a.

42. Ernst & Young LLP. *Supporting documentation for treatment guidelines for low back injuries.* Prepared for the California Workers' Compensation Institute, June 1996b.

43. Johnson, W. G., Baldwin, M. L., & Burton Jr., J. F. Why is the treatment of work-related injuries so costly? New evidence from California. *Inquiry* (Spring 1996).

44. Neuhauser, F. Report on the quality of treatment physician reports and cost-benefit presumption in favor of the treating physician. *Report to the Commission on Health and Safety and Workers' Compensation.* August, 1999.

45. Neuhauser, F. Medical cost, change of physician, and length of employer control. Memorandum to CHSWC and DIR, dated June 26, 2001.

46. Rice, T. (1997). Physician payment policies: Impacts and implications." *Annual Review of Public Health 18*: 549–65.

47. Swedlow, A., Johnson, G., Smithline, N., & Milstein, A. Increased costs and rates of use in California workers' compensation system as a result of self-referral by physicians. *New England Journal of Medicine*, 1992. 321(21): 1502–06.

48. WCIRB. *2000 California workers' compensation losses and expenses.* Report by the Workers' Compensation Insurance Rating Bureau of California, June 2001a.

49. Polakoff, P. L. Workplace injuries have become epidemic. *Workday Minnesota.* (Monday, 22 April 2002).

50. Rosenhan, D. (1973). On being sane in an insane place. *Science* 179: 250.

51. Feuerstein, M., & Beattie, P. Biobehavioral factors affecting pain and disability in low back pain: Mechanisms and assessment. *Phys. Ther.* 1995: 75: 267–280.

52. Waddell, G., McCulloch, J. A., Kummel, E., Venner, R. M. Nonorganic physical signs in low-back pain. *Spine*. 1980: 5: 193–203.

53. Collie, J. *Malingering and feigned sickness*. London: Edward Arnold Publishers Ltd. 1913.

54. Hoover, C. F. A new sign for the detection of malingering and functional paresis of the lower extremities. *JAMA*. 1908: 51: 746–747.

55. Lancourt, J., & Kettelhut, M. Predicting return to work for lower back pain patients receiving workers' compensation. *Spine*. 1992: 17: 629–640.

56. Waddell, G., & Richardson, J. Observation of overt pain behavior by physicians during routine clinical examination of patients with low back pain. *J. Psychosom. Res.* 1992 (Jan.): 36(1): 77–87.

57. Waddell, G. Clinical assessment of lumbar impairment. *Clin. Orthop.* 1987 Aug(221): 110–120.

58. Waddell, G., Bircher, M., Finlayson D., & Main, C. J. Symptoms and signs: Physical disease or illness behavior? *Br. Med. J.(Clin Res Ed)* 1984 Sep 22: 289 (6447): 739–41.

59. Waddell, G, Main, C. J., Morris, E. W., Di Paola, M., & Gray, I. C. Chronic low-back pain, psychologic distress, and illness behavior. *Spine* 1984 Mar: 9(2): 209–13.

60. Lande, R. G. Factitious disorders and the "professional patient." *J. Am. Osteopath Assoc.* 1996: 96(8): 468–72.

61. Main, C. J., & Waddell, G. Behavioral responses to examination: A reappraisal. of the interpretation of the "nonorganic signs." *Spine* 1998: 23(21): 2367–71.

62. Wipf, J. E., & Deyo, R. A. Low back pain. *Med. Clin North Amer.* 1995: 79(2): 232–46.

63. Keister, P. D., & Duke, A. D. Is it malingering, or is it "real"?: Eight signs that point to nonorganic back pain. *Postgrad Med.* 1999: 106(7): 77–84.

64. LaDou, J. The rise and fall of occupational medicine in the United States. *Am. J. Prev. Med.* 2002: 22(4): 285–295.

65. DePaolo, D. Help put an End to workers' comp malingering: A guide for business managers who face a workers' comp claim. *CFG Update.* (September/October) 1999: 10(4).

66. Phillips, K. A. Somatoform and factitious disorders. *Am. Fam. Phy.* 2000 June.

68. Ball, J. (1997). *The bible on workers' compensation investigations*. Thomas Investigative Publications.

69. Jackson, M. (2002). *Pain: The fifth vital sign*. New York: Crown Publishers.

70. Douglas, M. L. (2002). *Workers' compensation 101*. Waterford, PA: Douglas Publishers.

71. Shepard, B. (2001). *A war of nerves*. Cambridge, MA: Harvard University Press.

72. Pilowsky, I. (1997). *Abnormal illness behavior*. West Sussex, England: John Wiley & Sons Ltd.

73. Rogers, R. (Ed.). (1997). *Clinical assessment of malingering and deception*. New York: The Guilford Press.

74. Gatchel, R. J., & Turk, D. C. (Eds.). (1996). *Psychological approaches to pain*. New York: The Guilford Press.

75. Hadler, N. M. (1999). *Occupational musculoskeletal disorders*. Philadelphia, PA: Lippincott Williams & Wilkins.

76. Pankratz, L. (1998). *Patients who deceive*. Springfield, IL: Charles C. Thomas Publisher.

77. Kellner, R. (1986). *Somatization and hypochondriasis*. New York: Praeger Publishers.

78. Martin, W. T. (1989). *Problem employees and their personalities*. Westport, CT: Greenwood Press.

79. Simon, G. K., Jr. (2000). *In sheep's clothing*. Little Rock, AR: A. J. Christopher & Co.

80. Hall, H. V., & Poirier, J. G. (2001). *Detecting malingering and deception*. Boca Raton, FL: CRC Press LLC.

81. Hutchinson, G. L. (2001). *Disorders of simulation*. Madison, CT: Psychosocial Press.

82. Stoudemire, A. (1994). *Human Behavior* (2nd ed.). Philadelphia, PA: J. B. Lippincott.

83. Platt, F. W., & Gordon, G. H. (1999). *Field guide to the difficult patient interview*. Philadelphia, PA: Lippincott Williams & Wilkins.

84. Nance, J. (2000). *Conquering deception*. Kansas City, MO.

85. Link, C. R., & Staten, M. E. (1995). *Causes of litigation in workers' compensation programs*. Kalamazoo, MI: W. E. Upjohn Institute for Employment Research.

86. Randolph, D. C., & Ranavaya, M. I. Risk and disability in the workplace. In *State of the Art Reviews in Occupational Medicine*, vol. 25, no. 4 (Oct-Dec 2000). Philadelphia, PA: Hanley & Belfus, Inc.

87. Glucklich, A. (2001). *Sacred pain: Hurting the body for the sake of the soul*. London: Oxford University Press.

88. Jung, C. G. (1964). *Man and his symbols*. New York: Bantam Doubleday Dell Publishing Group.

89. Dimitrius, J-E., & Mazzarella. (1999). *Reading people*. New York: The Ballantine Publishing Group.

90. Rondinelli, R., & Katz, R. T. (Eval.) (2000). *Impairment rating and disability*. Philadelphia, PA: W. B. Saunders Company.

91. Samenow, S. E. (1984). *Inside the criminal mind*. New York: Times Books, A Division of Random House, Inc.

92. Dembe, A. E. (1996). *Occupation and disease*. New Haven, CT: Yale University Press.

93. Pace, N., Reville, R., Galway, L. et al. Improving the people's court: Issues facing the adjudication of claims before the California Workers' Compensation Appeals Board. Rand, DRU-2739-ICJ, January 2002.

94. Rice, T. Physician payment policies: Impacts and implications. 1997. *Ann. Rev. Pub. Health*: 18: 549–65.

95. Institute of Medicine. *Role of the primary care physician in occupational and environmental medicine*. Washington, DC: National Academy of Sciences: 1991.

96. Institute of Medicine. *Addressing the physician shortage in occupational and environmental medicine: Report of Study*. Washington, DC: National Academy of Sciences: 1991.

97. *Survey of workers' compensation laws*. 2002. The Alliance of American Insurers.

98. Prager, D. KRLA Radio. *The Dennis Prager Show*. 17 Dec. 2002.

99. Holloway, K. L., & Zerbe, K. J. Simplified approach to somatization disorder. *Postgrad Med.* 2000: 108(6): 89–95.

100. Blazer, D., Houpt, J. L. Perception of poor health in the healthy older adult. *J. AmGeriatr. Soc.*1979: 27: 330–334.

101. Shick Shadel Hospital. *The drug/alcohol reward system.* <http://www. Schick-shadel.com>.

102. Spieler,E. A., Barth, P. S., Burton, J. F., Jr., Himmelstein, J., & Rudolph, L. Recommendations to guide revision of the guides to the evaluation of permanent impairment. *JAMA.* 2000: 283: 519–523.

103. Clark, W. L., Haldeman, S., Johnson, P. et al. Back impairment and disability determinations, another attempt at objective, reliable rating. *Spine.* 1988:12: 332–341.

104. Nitschke, J. E., & Nattrass, C. L. et al. Reliability of the American Medical Association guides model for measuring spinal range of motion. Its implication for whole person impairment rating. *Spine.* 1999: Feb. 1: 24(3): 262-8.

105. Madson, T. J., Youdas, J. W., & Suman, V. J. Reproducibility of lumbar spine range of motion device. *J. Orth. Sports Physical Therapy.* 1999 Aug. 29(8): 470–7.

106. Mayer, R. S., Chen, I. H., & Lavender, S. A. et al. Variance in measurement of sagittal spine range of motion among examiners, subjects and instruments. *Spine* 1995 Jul 1: 20(13): 1489–93.

107. Nilsson, N., Hartvigsen, J., & Christensen, H. W. Normal ranges of passive cervical motion for women and men 20–60 years old. *J. Manipulative Physical Therapy* 1996 Jun: 19(5): 306–9.

108. Russell, P., Pearch, M. J., & Unsworth, A. A measurement of the range and coupled movements observed in the lumbar spine. *Br. J. Rheumatology* 1993 Jun: 32(6): 490–7.

109. Ensink, F. B., Saur, P.M., Frese, K., Seeger, D., & Hildebrandt, J. Lumbar range of motion: Influence of time of day and individual factors in measurements. *Spine* 1996 Jun 1: 21(11): 1339–43.

110. Poltras, S.,, Loisel, P., Prince, F., & Lemaire, J. Disability measurement in persons with back pain: Validity study of spinal range of motion and velocity. *Arch. Phys. Med. Rehabil.* 2000 Oct: 81(10): 1394–400.

111. McCarthy, M. L., McAndrew, M. P., & MacKenzie, E. J. Correlation between the measures of impairment, according to the modified system of the American Medical Association, and Function. *J. Bone Joint Surg. Am.* 1998 Jul: 80(7): 1034–42.

112. Rondinelli, R. D., Dunn, W., & Hassanein, K. M. A simulation of hand impairments: Efects on upper extremity function and implications toward medical impairment rating and disability determination. *Arch. Phys. Med. Rehabil.* 1997 Dec: 78(12): 1358–63.

113. W. V. Workers' Compensation Division HCAP. *Outpatient management of chronic pain*, 19 October 1996.

114. Insomnia: Assessment and management in primary care. *Sleep* vol. 22, Supplement 2. 1999.

115. California Workers' Compensation Institute Bulletin. October 31, 1997. No. 97–20.

116. O'Brien, David W. (Judge). Workers' Compensation Course Number 6. 2002. Covina, CA: Winterbrook Publishing Company.

117. WCRI—Permanent Partial Disability Benefits: Interstate Differences. Dr. Peter S. Barth and Michael Niss. September 1999. WC-99-2.

118. WCRI—Designing Benefit Structures for Temporary Disability: A Guide for Policymakers. Volumes 1 and 2. Dr. Richard B. Victor and Charles A. Fleischman. December 1989 WC-89-4/WC-89-4a.

119. *The guides to the evaluation of permanent impairment.* (4th ed.) Chicago, IL: American Medical Association. 2002. p. 2.

120. Cocciarella, L., Turk, M., & Andersson, G. Improving the evaluation of permanent impairment. *JAMA* 26 Jan 2000, vol. 283, no. 4.

121. Nugent, T., & Bernacki, E. Take this job and. . . . *Johns Hopkins Magazine* Nov. 2002: 54: No. 5.

122. Szasz. T. S., & Hollender, M. H. The basic models of the doctor-patient relationship. *Arch. Intern. Med.* 1956: 97: 585–92.

123. Quill, T. E. Partnerships in patient care: A contractual approach. *Ann. Intern. Med.* 1983: 98: 228–34.

124. Parson, T. (1951). *The Social System.* England: RKP.

125. WCIRB 2003 Report. Catalog No. AD1025A BB2003-01.

126. Syndenham, T. Dr. (1624–1689). *His life and original writings.* London: Wellcome Historical Medical Library, 1966.

127. Miller, T. R., & Levy, D. T. Geographic variation in expenditures for workers' compensation hospitalized claims. *Am. Journal Ind. Med.* 1999: 35(2): 103–111.

128. Tacci, J. A. et al. Clinical practices in the management of new-onset uncomplicated, low back workers' compensation disability claims. *Journal Occ. & Env. Med.* 1999: 41(5): 397–404.

129. Atlas, S. J. et al. Long-term disability and return to work among patients who have a herniated lumbar disk: The effect of disability compensation. *Journ. Of Bone and Joint Surg.-Amer.* 2000: vol. 82(1): 4–15.

130. What do injured workers think of their medical care? A survey conducted by the Division of Workers' Compensation State of California and The Survey Research Center University of California at Berkeley. 1997.

131. Himmelstein, J. S., & Pransky, G. Measuring and improving the quality of workers' compensation medical care. *John Burton's Workers' Compensation Monitor* (Nov/Dec 1995): 4–9.

132. Dembe, A. E., & Himmelstein, J. S. *New directions in workers' compensation medical care, in 1997–1998 workers' compensation managed care sourcebook—A practical guide to opportunities in the growing marketplace.* Faulkner & Gray, Inc.: 99–112.

133. Zenz, O., Dickerson, B., & Horvath, Jr., E. P. *Occupational medicine.* (3rd ed.). St. Louis, MO: Mosby-Year Book, Inc.

134. NCCI 2003 Data reporting workshop. 23–24 Jan 2003, Boca Raton, FL.

135. Hazlett, T. L., & Hummel, W. H. (1957). *Industrial medicine in western Pennsylvania.* Pittsburgh: University of Pittsburgh Press.

136. Freidson, E. (1970a). *Profession of medicine.* New York: Dodd, Mead.

137. Selleck, H. B., & Whittaker, A. H. (1962). *Occupational health in America*. Detroit: Wayne State University Press.

138. Ashford, N. A. (1976). *Crisis in the workplace*. Cambridge, MA: MIT Press.

139. Freedman, A. (1981). *Industry response to health risk*. New York: The Conference Board.

140. Taylor, P. J., & Raffle, P.A.B. (1981). *Preliminary periodic and other routine medical examinations*. *In Occupational Health Practice*. (2nd ed.). London: Butterworths.

141. Barnard, C. I. (1968). *The functions of the executive*. (30th anniversary ed.). Cambridge: Harvard University Press.

142. Taylor, F. W. (1911). *Principles of scientific management*. New York: Harper and Row.

143. Goldman, S. (ed.). (1953). *The words of Justice Brandeis*. New York: Henry Schuman.

144. Newkirk, W. L. Five events that changed occupational medicine. *Occupational Health Tracker*. 2001: 4(2).

145. Wilensky, H. L. (1967). *Organizational intelligence*. New York: Basic Books, Inc.

146. The scope of occupational medicine. ACOEM April 1992. *J. Occup. Med.* vol. 34(4).

147. Stevens, R. (1971). *American medicine and the public interest*. New Haven: Yale University Press.

148. Mechanic, D. (1976). *The growth of bureaucratic medicine*. New York: Wiley Interscience.

149. Perrow, C. (1977). *Complex organizations: A critical essay*. Glenview, IL: Scott, Foresman.

150. Scott, W. R. (1966). *Professionals in bureaucracies—Areas of conflict, professionalization*. Eds. Vollmer, H., & Mills, D. Englewood Cliffs, NJ: Prentice-Hall. pp. 265–91.

151. Davies, C. (1983). Professionals in bureaucracies: The conflict thesis revisited. In *The Sociology of Professions*. New York: St. Martin's.

152. Larson, M. S. (1977). *The rise of professionalism: A sociological analysis*. Berkeley: University of California Press.

153. Thompson, J. (1967). *Organizations in action*. New York: McGraw-Hill.

154. Derber, C. (1982). *Professionals as workers: Mental labor in advanced capitalism*. Boston: G. K. Hall.

155. Hamilton, A. (1943). *Exploring the dangerous trades*. Boston: Little, Brown & Company.

156. Walsh, D. C. (1987). *Corporate physicians*. New Haven: Yale University Press.

157. Wyatt, W. *The 2000/2001 Fifth Annual Survey*. Washington Business Group.

158. Gilpin, S. L. Making the case for disability management. *Risk and Insurance*. July 2001.

159. Ziegler, J. When it works. *Business and Health*. Feb 1999.

160. Strosahl, K. The new direction in disability management: Tactical teamwork. *Business & Health*. Dec 1998.

161. Lerner, J. R. The new direction in disability management. *Business & Health*. Oct 1998.

162. State Report Cards for Workers' Comp. 24 Feb 2003. Work Loss Data Institute.

163. Ramazzini, B. (1713). *De morbis artificum*. Chapter 2 of the Supplement. W. C. Wright (Trans.). London: Hafner Publishing Company, 1964.

164. Ballot, M. (1996). *Labor-management relations in a changing environment*. (2nd ed.). New York: John Wiley & Sons, Inc.

165. Dulles, F. R. (1949). *Labor in America*. Binghamton, NY: Vail-Ballou Press.

166. Franco, G. Ramazzini and workers' health. *Lancet* 1999: 354: 858–61.

167. Welch, D. M. Law talk. *Acupuncture Today*. Nov 2000.

168. Lencsis, P. M. (1998). *Workers' compensation: A reference and guide*. Westport, CT: Quorum Books, pp. 43–48.

169. O'Malley, T. J. Fighting insurance fraud for your client's sake. *Trial Magazine*. Dec 1998.

170. Attorney General's Office, Louisiana. November 9, 2001.

171. Westin, A. *Computers, health records, and citizens' rights*. Congressional Research Service. 60 (1976). Library of Congress.

172. *American Journal of Industrial Medicine*. 30(2): 130–141. 1996.

173. State of the Workers' Compensation Industry in California. April 2002. California Commission on Health and Safety and Workers' Compensation (CHSWC).

174. Legislative History and Achievements. California Coalition on Workers' Compensation (CCWC). 2000.

175. California: FLCs, *Workers' Comp*. *Rural Migration News*, 8(4), October 2002.

176. *Dorland's medical dictionary*. (28th ed.). Philadelphia, PA: W. B. Saunders Company, 1994.

177. Atkinson, W. The carpal tunnel conundrum. *Workforce*. September 2002.

178. Gardner, J. *Vocational rehabilitation in Florida's workers' compensation*. February 1988. WC-88-1. Workers' Compensation Research Institute.

179. Addley, K. *Occupational stress*. Oxford: Reed Educational and Professional Publishing Ltd. 1997.

180. McSwain, D. Businesses say insurance costs threaten existence. 2003. <http://www.businsgrp.com>

181. Zaidman, B. Vocational rehabilitation participation, duration and costs rise. Minnesota Department of Labor and Industry. December 2002.

182. U.S. Bureau of Census Website, Table 198. <http://www.census.gov/hhes/www/disable/cps/cps198.html>.

183. Victor, R. A., & Wang, D. Patterns and costs of physical medicine: Comparison of chiropractic and physician-directed care. December 2002. WC-02-07. WCRI.

184. Stoddard, S., Jans, L., & Kraus, L. (1998). *Chartbook on work and disability in the United States, 1998*. An InfoUse Report. Washington, DC: U.S. National Institute on Disability and Rehabilitation Research.

185. McNeil. (1997). *Americans with disabilities: 1994–95*. <http://www.census.gov./hhes/www/disable/html. Survey: SIPP, 1994–95.

186. U.S. Department of Labor, Bureau of Labor Statistics. *Local area unemployment statistics, current population survey, 2002.*

187. U.S. Department of Labor, Bureau of Labor Statistics, in cooperation with participating state agencies. *Survey of occupational injuries and illnesses, 2000.*

188. National Academy of Social Insurance. *Workers' compensation: Benefits, coverage, and costs, 2000 new estimates.* May 2002.

189. Workers' compensation state funds—what you don't know might hurt you. Conning Research & Consulting, Inc. <http://www.conningresearch.com.> April 2003.

190. *Physician's guide to medical practice in the California workers' compensation system.* California Industrial Medical Council. March 1994.

191. Kassirer, J. P. The use and abuse of practice profiles. *N. Engl. J. Med.* 1994: 330: 634–636.

192. Hanlon, C. R. Quality assessment and tracking results of cardiac surgery. *Ann. Thorac. Surg.* 1997: 64: 1560–1573.

193. Raphael, T. Happiness may be overrated. *Workforce.* May 2002.

194. Katon, W., Sullivan, M., & Walker, E. Medical symptoms without identified pathology: Relationship to psychiatric disorders, childhood and adult trauma, and personality traits. *Ann. Intern. Med.* 2001: 134: 917–925.

195. Van Korff, M., & Simon, G. The relationship between pain and depression. *Br. J. Psychiatry Suppl.* 1996: 101–108.

196. Szasz, T. S. (1974). *The myth of mental illness.* New York: Harper and Row Publishers, Inc.

197. McCunney, R. J. (1994). *A practical approach to occupational and environjmental medicine.* New York: Little Brown and Company.\

198. Little Hoover Commission Report. 1993. Report No. 120 workers Compensation: Containing the costs. February.

199. Mills, M. J., & Lipian, M. S. (1995). *Comprehensive textbook of psychiatry.* (6th ed.). Volume I. Baltimore: Williams & Wilkins, pp. 1614–1622.

200. Travin, S., & Protter, B. (1984). Malingering and malingering-like behavior: Some clinical and conceptual issues. *Psychiatric Quarterly,* 56(3): 189–197.

201. Culver, C. M., & Gert, B. (1982). *Philosophy in medicine: Conceptual and ethical issues in medicine and psychiatry.* New York: Oxford University Press.

202. Katz, L. (1996). *Ill-gotten gains: Evasion, blackmail, fraud, and kindred puzzles of the law.* Chicago: University of Chicago Press.

203. Ford, C. V. (1983). *The somatizing disorders. Illness as a way of life.* New York: Elsevier.

204. Balla, J. I., & Moraitis, S. Knights in armour: A follow-up of injuries after legal settlement. *Medical Journal of Australia* 2: 355–361.

205. American Psychiatric Association. *Diagnostic and statistical manual of mental disorders.* (4th ed.). Washington, DC: American Psychiatric Association, 1994. pp. 219–228.

206. Fabrega, H. (1978). *Disease and social behavior.* Cambridge, MA: MIT Press.

207. Stewart, M., Brown, J. B., Weston, W. W. et al. *Patient-centered medicine.* Thousand Oaks, CA: Sage Publications.

208. Ducatman, A. M. Occupational physicians and environmental medicine. *J. Occup. Med.* 1993: 35: 251–259.

209. Neas, L. M., Schwartz, J., & Dockery, D. A case-crossover analysis of air pollution and mortality in Philadelphia. *Environ. Health Perspect.* 107: 629–631. 1999.

210. Tong, S., Bagburst, P., McMichael, A. et al. Lifetime exposure to environmental lead and children's initelligence at 11–13 years: the Port Pirie cohort study. *Br. Med. J.* 312: 1569–1575 (1996).

211. Needleman, H. L., Riess, J. A., Tobin, M. J. et al. Bone lead levels and delinquent behavior. *JAMA* 1996: 275: 363–369.

212. Staessen, J. A., Roels, H. A., Emelianov, D. et al. Environmental exposures to cadmium, forearm bone density, and risk of fractures: Prospective population study. Public Health and Environmental Exposure to Cadmium (PheeCad) Study Group. *Lancet* 1999: 353: 1140–1144.

213. U.S. DHHS. Environmental Health. In *Healthy People 2010*, vol. 1. Washington, DC: U.S. Department of Health and Human Services. 2000: 8-1-8-40. Available: <http://www.health.gov/healthypeople/document/pdf/Volume1/08Environmental.pdf > [cited November 5 2002].

214. *Workers' compensation and the California economy*. April 2000. Commission on Health and Safety and Workers' Compensation for the State of California.

215. Bush, R. K. *The mystery of Illinois workers' compensation: Permanent partial disability*. May 2003. <http://www.ancelglink.com/indes.html>.

216. U.S. DOL Office of Disability Employment Policy. *The Workers' Compensation Crisis*. June 2003. http://www.dol.gov/odep.

217. Pope, C.A. et al. 2002. Lung cancer, cardiopulmonary mortality, and long-term exposure to fine particulate air pollution. Journ AMA 287:1132–1141.

218. Hong, Y.C. 2002. Effects of Air Pollutants on Acute Stroke Mortality. *Environmental Health Perspectives*. 110:187–191.

Index

Health Sciences Library
University of Saskatchewan Libraries
Room B205 Health Sciences Building
107 WIGGINS ROAD
SASKATOON, SK S7N 5E5 CANADA

About the Author

Richard E Sall MD received board certification in both General Surgery and Occupational Medicine. Before that, he had a two year tour of duty with the U.S. Army in Germany as a General Medical Officer with the Third Armored Cavalry. He has worked in varied settings throughout his career practicing occupational medicine from private practice and hospital based clinics to corporation medicine. Throughout his travels he noted a general need for an in-depth understanding of the workers' compensation system—hence the creation of this book.

The intent of this work is not to present a plethora of facts and figures but enable the reader to comprehend a difficult subject in regard to the cognitive practice of medicine.

He has four grown children and resides with his wife in Yorba Linda, California enjoying tennis as a hobby.